AN INTRODUCTORY STUDY GUIDE TO PUBLIC HEALTH AND EPIDEMIOLOGY

AN INTRODUCTORY STUDY GUIDE TO PUBLIC HEALTH AND EPIDEMIOLOGY

Nigel Unwin, Susan Carr and Joyce Leeson
with Tanja Pless-Mulloli

Open University Press
Buckingham • Philadelphia

Open University Press
Celtic Court
22 Ballmoor
Buckingham
MK18 1XW

and

1900 Frost Road, Suite 101
Bristol, PA 19007, USA

First Published 1997

A catalogue record of this book is available from the British Library

ISBN   0–335–15785–8   (pbk)   0–335–15786–6   (hbk)

Library of Congress Cataloging-in-Publication Data
Unwin, Nigel, 1958–
    Public health and epidemiology : a study guide for nurses / Nigel
Unwin, Susan M. Carr, and Joyce Leeson ; with Tanja Pless-Mulloli.
        p.   cm.
    Includes bibliographical references and index.
    ISBN 0–335–15786–6 (hbk)   ISBN 0–335–15785–8 (pbk)
    1. Public health—Outlines, syllabi, etc.   2. Public health
nursing—Outlines, syllabi, etc.   3. Epidemiology—Outlines,
syllabi, etc.   4. Test-taking skills.   I. Leeson, Joyce.   II. Carr,
Susan M., 1959– .   III. Title.
    [DNLM: 1. Public Health—examination questions.   2. Public Health—
nurses' instruction.   3. Epidemiology—examination questions.
4. Epidemiology—nurses' instruction.   WA 18.2 U62p   1992]
RA440.U49   1996
614 — dc20
DNLM/DLC
for Library of Congress   96–20503
                                                                                              CIP

Typeset by Graphicraft Typesetters Ltd., Hong Kong
Printed in Great Britain by St Edmundsbury Press Ltd,
Bury St Edmunds, Suffolk

CONTENTS

Contents

INTRODUCTION

People who practise public health come from many walks of life:

- nurses and doctors running a screening programme;
- local residents campaigning for better housing;
- engineers drilling bore holes to provide clean water for villagers in a developing country;
- politicians trying to introduce legislation to ban tobacco advertising;
- 'pop stars' who speak to school children on the dangers of drug misuse.

These are a few examples. Many people will not identify their activities as 'public health'. What links these and similar activities together is that each is at least partly, if not solely, concerned with protecting and improving the health of populations or communities. Such a broad range of activities illustrates that the factors which influence health are complex and wide-ranging. Any attempt to understand and change them must involve many disciplines, and the study of public health draws on the expertise of people from a variety of backgrounds. Statistics, psychology, sociology, microbiology, politics and management are some of the specialities which contribute to the study of public health. Epidemiology has a central role. It can be defined as the study of the distribution and determinants of health-related states and the application of this study to the control of health problems. Knowing the size of the health problems, who suffers from them and what causes them within a population is the basis for organized public health efforts to address them, as well as the means to know if the efforts were successful.

The focus of public health is on populations and communities. This is a very different perspective from the day-to-day focus of most health professionals on the health problems of individuals. We hope in this book to introduce students and practitioners of nursing to the 'public health perspective', to provide a framework for examining public health issues and to allow the reader to start to place her or his own practice within the wider context of the health, and determinants of health, of the community in which they work.

This book is a study guide. Our goal is to encourage you to think through, and be critical about, key issues to do with the measurement and improvement of public health and the role in this played by organized health care. The chapters cover topics which we hope will enable this goal to be achieved. There may be other areas you feel we should have covered. We would very much welcome your feedback on the content and any other aspect of this book.

How to use this book

Each chapter has a standard format and is presented in the following way.

- *Questions*: some examples of the kinds of questions the chapter will help you to answer.
- *Outcomes*: what you should be able to do after working through the chapter and the exercises provided.
- *Exercises*: these are presented throughout the chapter. They are there to help you understand key issues. It is therefore important to work through them. You'll be pleased to hear that most of them are very short. There are a few exercises that will involve going away and seeking out other information, but these are identified in the text and are optional. They are there if you wish to develop further your understanding of a particular issue.
- *Summary*: key issues, ideas or concepts from the chapter are identified in summary questions. Spaces are left for your responses for two main reasons: (a) by completing this section you can revise the issues of the chapter and assess yourself on how well you have met the outcomes; (b) you can make your own summary specific to your particular health interests and the branch of health care.
- *Suggested reading*: at the back of the book we have identified for each chapter some useful references for further reading.

An overview of the book: brief summaries of the chapters

Chapter 1, 'Critical use of routinely available health information', starts by considering the types of routinely available information which are relevant to public health. Criteria are suggested by which to assess critically the quality of routinely available health information. The application of these criteria is illustrated by consideration of routinely available information on population size and cause of death. Next, the types of information routinely available on morbidity (episodes of illness) are considered, and the concept of the 'health care iceberg' is introduced. Finally, consideration is given to the potential pitfalls when one is making comparisons between the health of populations in different places or at different times using routinely collected information.

Chapter 2, 'Measuring the frequency of health problems', starts by illustrating the need for rates to measure the frequency of health problems. Two rates of special importance in epidemiology, incidence and prevalence, are defined and the relationship between them is discussed. The rest of the chapter uses mortality rates (because these tend to be the most widely

used indicators of the 'health' of a population) as an example to illustrate
what is meant by crude, specific and standardized rates. Finally, calculation
of age standardized rates by both the direct and indirect methods is illustrated, and the potential shortcomings of both approaches are discussed.

Two of the main aims of epidemiology are to identify possible causes of
disease and to estimate the potential improvement in a population's health
if such causes were removed. Measures of 'relative risk' (and the identification of 'risk factors') and 'attributable risk' respectively are the main methods
by which these aims are met. Chapter 3, 'Measures of risk', illustrates the
meaning of these terms and seeks to encourage a critical approach to their
use and interpretation.

Chapter 4, 'Epidemiological study designs', provides an overview of the
approaches (study designs) used in epidemiology to measure the amount
of a disease or health state in a population and to identify possible causes
of a disease or health state. A classification of the different study designs
is given and each is described. Emphasis is given to the strengths and weaknesses of the different types of study.

Chapter 5, 'Weighing up the evidence from epidemiological studies',
is all about interpreting the results from epidemiological studies. An association between a disease or health state and possible cause may not be
real but owing to 'bias', 'confounding' or 'chance'. These terms are defined
and illustrated, and methods for addressing them in the design and analysis
of epidemiological studies are discussed. Finally, even if an association is
real is does not necessarily follow that it is 'causal'. What is meant when
we describe something as a 'cause' of a disease or health state is discussed
and criteria are suggested by which causality can be assessed.

Chapter 6, 'The determinants of health and disease', compares the major
causes of death between the past and today in developed countries, and
compares the main causes of death in developing and developed countries that exist now. The concepts of the 'demographic and health transitions' are introduced. The concepts of 'causes' and 'determinants' of
diseases and health states are discussed. The fact that determinants of
health can be seen to operate on many levels, from the political and
economic spheres through to individual lifestyles and down to the level
of cell biology, is discussed as is the interrelationship between these different levels. The importance of the macroeconomic environment as a
determinant of a population's health is given particular emphasis.

Chapter 7, 'Health promotion', describes the different types of activity
which come under the heading of health promotion. Health education is
one of the activities coming under the umbrella of health promotion to
which health care workers often contribute. Five different approaches, or
models, of health education or health promotion are discussed. The reader
is encouraged to consider critically where the balance between individual
and collective responsibility for health should lie.

A consideration of the term 'health needs assessment' (Chapter 8) begs
the questions of what is meant by 'health' and what is meant by 'need'?
The chapter begins by addressing both these questions. A classification of
need is given. Chapter 6 illustrates that determinants of health can be seen
to operate on many levels and similarly health needs can be identified on
many levels. A particular example of health needs assessment is community

health profiling. What is meant by this and how it might be approached is discussed, and a framework for constructing a community health profile is suggested.

Screening individuals to prevent or cure a disease is a deceptively attractive idea. Increasing numbers of health care workers are being asked to undertake screening as part of their day-to-day work. However, a poorly thought out and implemented screening programme may be ineffective or worse still, harmful. Chapter 9, 'Principles of screening', considers the rationale and criteria for selecting a condition to be targeted in a screening programme. It also considers some of the factors which contribute to the successful implementation of a screening programme.

Chapters 10 and 11 consider the effectiveness of health care. Chapter 10, 'The effectiveness of health care: a historical perspective', is devoted to a historical perspective because this provides an extremely salutary lesson on the assumed effectiveness of health care and should lead us to question critically the effectiveness of health care today. First, the terms 'efficacy', 'effectiveness' and 'efficiency' are discussed and defined. Then the common assumption that the huge improvements in health which occurred in developed countries, such as those of Western Europe and North America, over the past 150 years were mainly owing to advances in medical science is addressed. A critical examination of the evidence, discussed in this chapter, shows that this assumption is wrong. The main factors which led to improvements in health and the part played by public health measures are discussed.

Chapter 11, 'Assessing the effectiveness of health care today', follows on from Chapter 10 by beginning with a discussion of the effectiveness of health care today. Criteria are suggested for helping to decide whether a particular health service is effective, and it is noted that an effective service needs to do much more than simply provide efficacious treatments. Approaches to evaluating the effectiveness of a service and the strengths and weaknesses of different kinds of health service information in assisting with evaluation are discussed. Finally, the reasons why evidence on effectiveness is often ignored by those providing health services and how this situation may be remedied are addressed.

CHAPTER 1

CRITICAL USE OF ROUTINELY AVAILABLE HEALTH INFORMATION

What types of information relevant to health are routinely available?

How should the quality of routinely available health information be judged?

What is meant by the 'health care iceberg'?

What cautions need to be exercised in comparing differences in health over time or between places using routine information sources?

After working through this chapter, you should be able to:

• describe the types of routinely available health information;

• provide a set of guidelines on the critical use of routinely available health information;

• describe the processes by which routinely available information on population size and deaths is collected, collated and disseminated;

• describe some of the different types of information available on morbidity and their shortcomings;

• discuss the concept of the 'health care iceberg';

• compare critically health information collected in different places or at different points in time.

What types of health information do we need and what is routinely available?

Public health is concerned with the protection and the improvement of the health of populations and communities. Profiling of the health needs of a community (considered in detail in Chapter 8) is an essential first step in this activity, and to do this we need at least three types of information. These are:

- information to describe basic characteristics of the community, such as numbers of individuals by age and sex;
- information to describe and monitor the health status of the community;
- information on the determinants of health in the community ('determinants' refers to any factors which can bring about a change in health, for better or worse, and are considered in detail in Chapter 6).

Consider the types of information that might be needed to describe the health status and determinants of health of a community by working through Exercise 1.1.

Consider the local area in which you live: depending on your circumstances this might mean a street of houses, a hall of residence or a block of flats. You have been asked to describe the health and the determinants of health for residents in your street, hall or block. List the information you would seek:

1 To describe the health of the residents.

2 To describe the determinants (influences on) the health of the residents (you could break this down into influences to do with the individual; with the local social, economic and physical environment; and with the wider social, economic and physical environment).

In describing the health status of residents in your area in Exercise 1.1, you may have mentioned deaths and causes of death and episodes of illness. You may also have mentioned more positive aspects of health, perhaps trying to get at general well being and quality of life.

Factors you may have considered under 'determinants' include:

- *Influences to do with the individual*: e.g. 'lifestyle' factors, such as smoking, diet and exercise; knowledge and attitudes to health issues; wealth, employment and educational background; personality and response to stressful situations.
- *Influences to do with the local social, economic and physical environment*: e.g. levels of crime and vandalism; the quality of housing; access to health care; access to good food; access to leisure facilities; levels of traffic and road traffic accidents; employment and educational opportunities in the area; levels of air pollution.
- *Influences to do with the wider social, economic and physical environment*: e.g. advertising and pricing policy on tobacco and alcohol; road safety legislation; legislation on contraception and abortion; national economic and employment policy; the effects of greenhouse gases and global warming.

We have covered some of the information we might like to collect to describe the health status of a community and the factors influencing that community's health. How much of this information is routinely available? 'Routinely available' refers to information which is collected, collated (put together and analysed) and disseminated on a regular basis. The answer, of course, depends partly on where you are. Table 1.1 gives an overview of information relevant to health that was found to be routinely available in Manchester, England, in 1992. It includes nationally produced 'health' (deaths and disease notifications) statistics, as well as statistics available from the local health authority and local government. Table 1.2 gives the definitions of some routinely available and commonly used 'vital statistics'. (Issues to do with the use and interpretation of rates are discussed in detail in Chapter 2.) Death rates, in particular, tend to be used as a proxy for a community's health and we shall examine the compilation and use of these in greater detail.

Table 1.1 Examples (these are far from all) of routinely available information relevant to health (based on the situation in Manchester, England, in 1992)

Description	Source
Demographic information	
Census information (includes numbers by age, sex and ethnicity, type of employment, educational level, house tenure, overcrowding) for the area.	Office of Population Censuses and Surveys (OPCS), available through local government and health authorities.
Births: details of all births registered in area, including birth weight and occupation of mother etc.	OPCS, available through health authority information departments.
Deaths: details of all deaths registered in the area, such as age, cause of death, place of death, occupation of deceased.	OPCS, available through health authority information departments.
Population estimates and projections: estimates of population size between censuses, projected population size in future.	OPCS, available through local health authority information departments.

Table 1.1 cont'd

Description	Source
Vital statistics	
Rates of deaths, including perinatal and infant mortality, birth rates and fertility rates (these are shown in more detail in Table 1.2).	OPCS, available through local health authority information departments.
Morbidity	
Notifiable diseases: infectious disease notifications by age, sex, address, date, organism.	Infection control and surveillance unit, Manchester City Council.
Cancer registrations: diagnosis, age, sex, occupation, area of residence, details of treatment.	Centre for cancer epidemiology, Christie Hospital, Manchester.
Hospital discharges: by age, sex, method of admission, diagnosis, operative procedures etc.	Information department of local health authority.
Socio-economic data	
Unemployment benefit: numbers claiming by area.	Manchester City Council.
Free school meals: numbers claiming by area.	Manchester City Council.
Housing benefit: numbers claiming by area.	Manchester City Council.
Income support: numbers claiming by area.	Manchester City Council.
Environmental data	
Road accidents: casualties and type of accident by area (police division); only includes accidents to which police called.	Greater Manchester Transportation Unit.
Crime statistics: numbers and type of reported crime by area.	Greater Manchester Police.
Air pollution: results from different monitoring sites around the city.	Environmental health department, Manchester City Council.
Drinking water: levels of lead and coliform bacteria by water supply zones.	Environmental health department, Manchester City Council.
Noise: Number of complaints.	Environmental health department, Manchester City Council.
Pests: Number of complaints for cockroaches, rats etc.	Environmental health department, Manchester City Council.

Source: J. Lord (1992) *A Guide to Data Sources in Manchester*. Manchester Public Health and Human Resource Centre.

Using information critically

As Tables 1.1 and 1.2 show, there is potentially a lot of information around which is relevant to health. The information which is available, however, is a very mixed bag, of varying quality and usefulness. Any source of information must be used critically. Here are four areas you should consider:

Table 1.2 Definitions of some commonly used and readily available vital statistics

Statistic	Definition
Births and fertility	
Crude birth rate	Number of live births to residents of an area in one year per 1000 population of that area (usually based on the population present at the mid-year).
General fertility rate	Number of live births to residents of an area in one year per 1000 female population aged 15–44 years in that area.
Total period fertility rate	Average number of children per woman based on current fertility rates.
Mortality	
Perinatal mortality rate	Number of still births and deaths within the first week of life per 1000 total births (live and still).
Infant mortality rate	Number of deaths in children under one year per 1000 live births.
Crude death rate	Number of deaths to residents of an area in one year per 1000 population of that area.
Age-specific death rate	Number of deaths to residents of an area in one age group in one year per 1000 population in that age group.
Cause-specific death rate	Number of deaths to residents of an area from a specific cause in one year per 1000 population.

- *Accuracy.* Inaccuracies can arise at several points. For example, if the information is based on hospital records, how accurate was the original information, and how accurately was that information coded, transcribed and turned into routine statistics?
- *Completeness.* Completeness refers to completeness of the information recorded on each person as well as whether everyone (or every event) is included who should be.
- *Timeliness.* How up to date is the information? How up to date the information needs to be depends on what you want to use it for. Information one or two years old on the size and characteristics of a population is likely still to be perfectly acceptable (barring major social upheaval over that time) to describe such things as the profile of age, sex, ethnic mix, types of housing and so on. Information of this age to monitor levels of food poisoning would be useless – the picture could easily have changed over this time, but more importantly the time scale would be far too long to allow effective preventive action to be taken.
- *Validity or appropriateness.* Finally, you should ask whether the information is valid or appropriate for what you are trying to find out. If you were interested in the amount of lung cancer in the community, then looking at deaths from lung cancer should give a reasonable idea because most people with lung cancer die from it within a fairly short space of time. What if you were interested in the amount of diabetes in the community? Deaths from diabetes would give a very poor impression of this. Diabetes is a chronic condition with very long average

duration. Although the majority of people with diabetes die from one of its complications (especially if one includes coronary heart disease), diabetes is frequently not recorded as a cause of death.

Consider the issues of accuracy, completeness, timeliness and validity for an information source with which you are familiar in Exercise 1.2.

Exercise **1.2**

As a health care worker you are a collector of health information, contributions to patient or client records are one example. Choose one of the areas to which you have contributed. Write below what you know about the accuracy, completeness and timeliness of the information.

Could this information source be used to help build up a picture of the health of the local community? Give your reasons, including reservations you may have about the use of the information in this way.

We now turn to consider three types of very commonly used information in more detail.

Census information

A census is a count (an enumeration, to use the more technical term) of the population. One of the most famous censuses is that reported in the New Testament following a 'decree from Caesar Augustus that all the world should be enrolled', and for which Mary and Joseph travelled to Bethlehem.

Most industrialized, and many developing non-industrialized, countries undertake regular censuses of their populations. The usual aim of census enumeration is to record the identity of every person in every place of residence, including their age or date of birth, sex, marital status and occupation. Other personal details may also be recorded, such as place of birth, race or ethnicity, educational history and literacy. Details on living conditions, such as the number of rooms in the house and the type of toilet, are also frequently collected. In most countries the census is the main source of information on the size, age and sex structure and basic socio-economic characteristics of the population.

As an example we will describe the census in the United Kingdom. Regular ten-yearly censuses have been carried out since 1801, with one omission in 1941 (in the midst of the Second World War). A government department, called the Office of Population Censuses and Surveys (OPCS), is responsible for conduct of the census, and for the collation, analysis and dissemination of information from the census. During the 1991 census, information was collected about households, as well as about individuals. Data were, for example, obtained on age, sex, marital status, occupation and employment, education, car ownership, housing tenure and the presence of long-term illness.

For the administration of the census the whole country is divided into enumeration districts (in other countries similar administrative units are often called 'census tracts'). On average, each enumeration district contains about 200 households. An enumerator is responsible for ensuring that a form is delivered to every household prior to the night of the census and is collected from that household as soon after the census as possible. The head of the household is required by law to provide details on the census form for every person who is a member of the household, present or absent, on the night of the census. Now that you know a little about the census in the UK and how it is conducted think through some of the issues of accuracy, completeness and timeliness.

Exercise 1.3

Under the following headings suggest potential shortcomings of census information.

Accuracy

Completeness

Timeliness

The accuracy of the information is dependent on the people completing the form, i.e. the heads of households. The head of a household may not be familiar with all the details required on other individuals in the household. He or she may use vague terms for such items as occupation, making it difficult to put the individuals into a definite occupational category when the OPCS comes to code and analyse the data. The census aims to count every person living in the United Kingdom on the night of the census. It obtains information about those not present at their residence from the head of the household. However, some people will not be counted in a census and others will be counted twice. In terms of health needs, a major concern is those people without a permanent address; for example, those living in bed and breakfast accommodation and those sleeping rough. We know that these people have specific health needs, but the census will only count a small proportion of them. Despite the legal requirement, some people, particularly in inner-city areas, may refuse to complete the census form. For example, it has been estimated that almost a third of young men were missed in some inner-city areas of London in the 1991 census. Finally, in terms of timeliness it is a major drawback of the census that it occurs only once every ten years. Estimates of the population between censuses are based on births, deaths and migrations. The first two are accurately known, but internal migration (i.e. within the UK) is very hard to track, so population estimates for small areas may become very inaccurate over this time. Similarly, the social and economic fabric of an area can change markedly over ten years. Recently, in response these problems of timeliness, samples of 10 per cent of the population have been taken in between the ten-yearly censuses.

Information on causes of death

Statistics on death rates and causes of death are one of the main sources used to describe the state of health of a population or community. Before we look at some of the obvious potential shortcomings of using mortality data as a main measure of the health of a community, let us examine how this information is derived. Again the situation in the UK will be used as an example, although the system is very similar in most industrialized countries.

In the UK since 1874 it has been a legal requirement that all births and deaths are registered. As for the census, the system for doing this is organized by the OPCS. Throughout the country is a network of Registry Offices, each headed by a local registrar, where information on all births and deaths occurring in that area are collected. When a death occurs the registered medical practitioner who attended the deceased during the final illness is required by law to issue a medical certificate of the cause of death. There is an internationally agreed format for recording the cause of death, used in the UK and many other countries. This is illustrated in Figure 1.1. The medical practitioner is asked to distinguish between 'immediate cause of death', which is that given in section 1(a) of the death certificate (see Figure 1.1), and 'underlying cause of death', which is given by the lowest completed part of section 1. This is an important distinction. Underlying cause of death can be defined as: the disease or injury which initiated the train of events leading to death; or, if the immediate cause of death was an injury, the circumstances of the accident or violence that produced the fatal injury.

1 (a) Disease or condition directly leading to death _____

  (b) Other disease or condition, if any, leading to 1(a) _____

  (c) Other disease or condition, if any, leading to 1(b) _____

2 Other significant conditions contributing to the death but not related to the disease or condition causing it _____

Figure 1.1   Internationally agreed format for indicating cause of death on death certificates.

The medical practitioner gives the death certificate to a 'qualified inform-ant'. This is usually a close relative of the deceased but could also be some-one like the person in charge of a rest home if that is where the deceased last resided. It is the responsibility of the qualified informant to take the death certificate to the local Registry Office to register the death. When the informant hands in the doctor's death certificate, he or she will also be asked to provide the following information on the deceased: date and place of death; sex; usual address; full name, and maiden name if a married woman; date and place of birth; occupation. If the registrar is satisfied (in some cases, such as a death in suspicious circumstances, the case may need to go to a coroner for cause of death to be determined) then all these details are forwarded to the OPCS.

At the OPCS each piece of information is given a numerical code and transferred to a computer for analysis. Cause of death is coded following an internationally agreed system, called the International Classification of Disease (or ICD for short). Statistics on cause of death are almost always based on the underlying cause. The whole process, from death to becom-ing a mortality statistic, is summarized in Figure 1.2.

Now that you have read how cause of death statistics are derived, give some thought to potential problems with their quality in Exercise 1.4.

Exercise 1.4

Under the following headings suggest potential shortcomings of cause of death information.

Accuracy

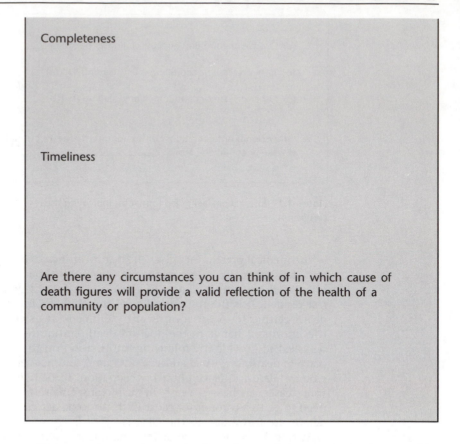

Completeness

Timeliness

Are there any circumstances you can think of in which cause of death figures will provide a valid reflection of the health of a community or population?

There are two major areas where inaccuracies can occur in mortality data. One is in ascribing cause of death. It can often be very difficult to ascribe a single cause of death, never mind trying to break it down into a sequence of events from an underlying cause leading to the immediate cause. This is especially true in elderly people, where the presence of several disease processes at once is quite possible. It is generally the case that with increasing age of the deceased the accuracy of the recorded cause of death decreases. The other major area for inaccuracies is in the information received by the registrar from the qualified informant. The accuracy of the information given will depend on how well the informant knew the deceased, and may also be affected by his or her emotional state at the time. It is known, for example, that there can be an almost natural tendency to emphasize at such a time the importance of the deceased, which could result in his or her occupation being embellished.

One of the advantages of death statistics, at least in most industrialized countries, compared to other forms of health statistics is that they are virtually 100 per cent complete. In many developing countries deaths are very incompletely registered, and in such situations special studies need to be undertaken to get accurate estimates of death rates and cause of death. In terms of timeliness it depends on their use. Mortality statistics in the UK, for example, appear within one year (or less) of being collected.

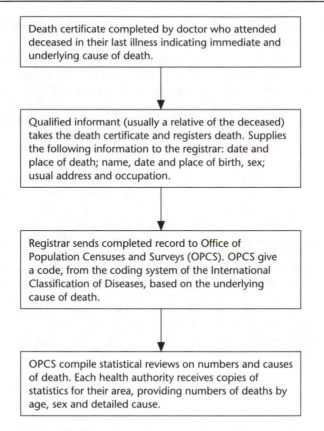

Death certificate completed by doctor who attended deceased in their last illness indicating immediate and underlying cause of death.

Qualified informant (usually a relative of the deceased) takes the death certificate and registers death. Supplies the following information to the registrar: date and place of death; name, date and place of birth, sex; usual address and occupation.

Registrar sends completed record to Office of Population Censuses and Surveys (OPCS). OPCS give a code, from the coding system of the International Classification of Diseases, based on the underlying cause of death.

OPCS compile statistical reviews on numbers and causes of death. Each health authority receives copies of statistics for their area, providing numbers of deaths by age, sex and detailed cause.

Figure 1.2 A summary of how mortality statistics are collected, collated and disseminated in England and Wales.

This is quite adequate for most uses. However, obviously if you were using mortality statistics to identify epidemics of infectious diseases to which you wanted to make a rapid response, such as a cholera outbreak, a year would be most untimely.

Finally, what were your views in Exercise 1.4 on the use of cause of death figures as a reflection of the health of a community? You may have answered that mortality can never adequately indicate health because health is much more than the absence of disease. This is a fair viewpoint. However, it can also be argued that where death rates are very high, as they are in all ages in sub-Saharan Africa, this is at least a good indication that health is also very poor. Arguably in this situation, cause of death patterns also give a good indication of cause of ill health patterns: the main causes of death – gastrointestinal infections, malaria etc. – are also the main causes of ill health. In industrialized countries, however, cause of death patterns give a very distorted picture of patterns of ill health; for example, very few deaths are recorded as being owing to mental illness or degenerative joint disease, two of the major causes of ill health in industrialized countries.

Information on the causes of morbidity and the health care iceberg

Routinely available information on morbidity comes mainly from data on the activity of health services. In theory such information ought to provide a much better indication of the causes of ill health in a community than information on mortality. Unfortunately, this promise is rarely realized. The types of morbidity data which are available vary greatly between different countries, tend to change as health care structures change and are changing in response to improvements in computer systems to handle the information.

The aim here, therefore, is not to describe any of the systems for collecting morbidity in detail but to highlight issues in the use and interpretation of such information. One issue which is common to any data source based on health care activity is what has been called the health care iceberg. This is illustrated in Figure 1.3. People admitted to hospital represent only the tip of the iceberg of all people who are ill in the community. Even the use of contacts with primary health care will miss a large proportion of people who are ill but who may not seek help or may seek the advice of friends, relatives, pharmacists or alternative therapists rather than members of the primary health care team.

As examples we will briefly consider the three sources of routinely available morbidity data listed in Table 1.1. These examples are thus based on the situation in the UK.

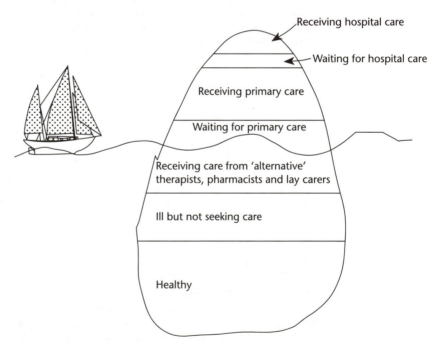

Figure 1.3   Illustration of the health care 'iceberg'.
Source: Based on an illustration in Donaldson and Donaldson (1983) *Essential Community Medicine*, MTP Press.

Infectious disease notification. Doctors are required by law to inform the local medical officer for infectious disease control if they suspect that a patient is suffering from one of around 30 notifiable diseases. These diseases include measles, meningitis, tuberculosis, whooping cough, cholera and food poisoning. The aim of this system is to allow the local medical officer to take appropriate action to prevent further cases of the disease. The medical officer is also responsible for collating and monitoring the notifications, and for sending the local figures to a national centre which regularly publishes statistics on trends in infectious disease notifications. Unfortunately, although it is a legal requirement and doctors are paid a small fee for notifying, underreporting is very common. Even with diseases which almost always require hospitalization, such as meningococcal meningitis, up to 50 per cent of cases may not be reported. In addition, many notifications are based on a suspicion that the person has the disease, and this may not be followed up by confirmatory laboratory tests. Thus notifications tend to be incomplete and many will be inaccurate. Despite this they seem to be adequate for following major trends and identifying outbreaks, the assumption being that if levels of underreporting and accuracy remain the same, then changes in the number of notifications represent real changes in the amount of disease.

Cancer registration. Disease registers, which ideally contain the details of every person with a particular disease living in a geographically defined area, offer many potential rewards by providing high-quality information for research, planning and patient management. Examples of diseases for which registers exist in some areas include diabetes, coronary heart disease and cancers. Cancer registries exist in many countries. A national cancer registration scheme was set up in the UK in 1962, and in each area of the country there is a cancer registry covering a population usually of several million people. Cancer registration is not a legal requirement and the registry depends upon the cooperation of local doctors to inform them of patients with cancer. The registry also receives copies of death certificates of residents in its area on which cancer was mentioned as a cause of death. Registers require a huge amount of work, first to try to identify every individual with the disease in the area, and second to keep the details of those on the register up to date. Studies of cancer registries in the UK suggest that underreporting can be large, but that for those cases on the register the accuracy of the information is high.

Hospital inpatient activity in the UK is currently recorded as hospital episode statistics. An episode of treatment refers to a period care received under one particular hospital consultant. If an individual is transferred to the care of another consultant, this counts as a new episode. If an individual was discharged and readmitted ten times in one year this would be recorded as ten episodes and would be indistinguishable on the statistics from ten individuals each admitted once. Thus episodes of care, not individuals, are the basic unit being counted. From each hospital, a minimum data set for each episode is sent to the Department of Health for collation into national statistics on hospital activity. Data collected in the hospital episode information system include the speciality of the consultant under whose care the episode took place, the clinical diagnosis, the admission and discharge date, the referring general practitioner and the age, sex and usual address of the patient. Hospital episode statistics are a potentially very useful source of information about illnesses treated in hospital. Their actual usefulness to provide a basis for the assessment of health service needs has been disputed, however, mainly because of the quality of the diagnostic information and its completeness. In addition, activity in private hospitals is not included, though in some areas it is a substantial part of the health care used by residents.

This brief overview of morbidity data illustrates some of the major problems in its collection and use. Completeness and accuracy are recurring themes, and a striking drawback of hospital activity data is that episodes are counted rather than individuals. You have probably also picked up from the discussion of the three examples above that the systems are quite separate. Being able to link these systems together routinely (this can be done at huge effort in 'one-off' studies) would provide some major advantages. This is called *record linkage*. It would require that each individual has a unique and reliable personal identifier, such as an ID number. This identifier would have to be used on every information system, whether for disease notification, disease registration, hospital admissions or death registration. All of these information systems would then need to be brought together (which in practical terms means on the same computer system in a common format). With such a system it would be possible to do such things as count the number of sick individuals in a population based on the information available and to follow individuals through courses of hospital treatment. In some countries individuals are given a unique identifying number at birth, which is then used on all health records. This greatly facilitates record linkage, and even without routinely bringing all the data together on to one system, *ad hoc* record linkage studies are much easier. Of course, being able to link individuals' records together in this way also raises huge ethical and political issues, to do with patient confidentiality and potential abuses of the information.

Comparing routinely collected information over time and between areas

The main aim of this chapter has been to try to show the importance of a critical (some might even say sceptical) approach to using routinely available health information. Let us finish off with a very common scenario: making comparisons between areas, or over time. A good idea in using any information source is to try to think through the process involved, from the data being collected to their being presented in their current form. Try to identify each step in the process and ask yourself what errors could arise at each step. Try doing this now when answering the questions in Exercise 1.5.

In the following hypothetical comparisons, assume that in reality there is no difference in the frequency of the disease. Try to think of some possible explanations for the apparent differences.

1 In Germany, the frequency of low blood pressure, based on hospital activity data, is greater than in the UK.

2 In the City of Manchester, there has been a 50 per cent increase in food poisoning notifications over six months.

3 Based on cancer registration data, one area of the UK has a higher rate of bowel cancer than another area.

4 In two neighbouring health districts, death rates from diabetes are substantially higher in one than in the other.

For each of the hypothetical comparisons in Exercise 1.5 there are several possible explanations. Here are some suggestions.

1 Differences in diagnostic practice: doctors in Germany tend to diagnose and treat low blood pressure at levels that would be considered normal in the UK. Differences in ascertainment: assuming that diagnostic practices are the same, perhaps more people have their blood pressure checked in Germany. Differences in place of treatment: remember that these are hospital data; perhaps in the UK more people are treated by their general practitioner, whereas in Germany people tend to be admitted to hospital for treatment. Differences in the frequency of hospital admission: assuming that the situation is the same in Germany and that the hospital data represent episodes rather than individuals, perhaps there are more admissions to hospital per person in Germany.

2 Assuming that levels of food poisoning in the city have stayed the same, then the most likely explanation is an increase in ascertainment. Perhaps the local medical officer recently ran a campaign to encourage all doctors to notify cases of food poisoning.
3 The most likely explanation is that in the area with the lower rate, fewer of the cases are being notified to the cancer registry.
4 Remember that cause of death is based on the underlying cause given on the death certificate. A possible explanation is that in the district with the higher rate there is a team with a special interest in diabetes. For someone with diabetes who dies of an immediate cause only possibly related to diabetes, they tend to record it as the underlying cause of death, whereas in the other district diabetes would not be given as the underlying cause in this situation.

Summary

Write your own summary of this chapter by answering the following questions.

1 Summarize the range of routinely available information which may be useful in describing the health and determinants of health of a community or population.

2 Suggest four criteria with which to assess critically any information source.

3 Identify the main potential sources of error in information on cause of death and the details of the deceased.

4 Describe what is meant by the term record linkage, and how this might be organized.

5 What is meant by the 'health care iceberg'?

6 Summarize some of the issues to be considered when comparing disease rates based on routine information sources over time or between places.

MEASURING THE FREQUENCY OF HEALTH PROBLEMS

> What are rates and why are they needed?
>
> What are incidence and prevalence and how are they related?
>
> Why are standardized rates needed and how are they produced?

After working through this chapter you should be able to:

- discuss the need for rates;

- explain what a rate is;

- define incidence and prevalence;

- describe the relationship between incidence and prevalence;

- describe what is meant by crude, specific and standardized rates;

- describe what is meant by crude, specific and standardized mortality rates;

- understand how directly and indirectly age standardized rates are derived;

- appreciate the potential shortcomings of both indirect and direct methods of standardization.

Why are rates needed?

Work through Exercise 2.1.

Over the course of seven years 146 people were referred to a hospital plastic surgery unit because they had been bitten by dogs. Details of the breeds of dog causing the bites were collected from 107 people. The main breeds responsible were as follows:

Staffordshire bull terrier	15 cases
Jack Russell	13 cases
Medium-sized mongrel	10 cases
Alsatian	9 cases
Labrador	8 cases
Collie	6 cases

Question: Does this mean that Staffordshire bull terriers are more likely to bite people than collies?

If your answer is 'no', or perhaps 'not sure', what other information would you like before you could answer this question properly?

Source of figures: P.C. Shewell and J.D. Nancarrow (1991) Dogs that bite. *British Medical Journal*, 303, 1512–13.

We hope you agree that it does not follow from the information in Exercise 2.1 that Staffordshire bull terriers are more likely to bite people than collies. Further information is required. Two pieces of information you may have thought of are: how many dogs are there in each breed, and how much time do those dogs spend around people? It is possible that collies are more likely to bite than Staffordshire bull terriers. This would be compatible with the results above if Staffordshire bull terriers were much less common or spent less time with people. So to make a valid comparison we need to relate the number of bites for each breed to the number of dogs in that breed, or to the amount of time the dogs spend with people. In other words, we need to use *rates*.

What is a rate?

A rate is a measure of how frequently an event occurs. All rates are ratios, which simply means that they consist of one number divided by another number. The top number is called the *numerator* and the bottom the *denominator*. The numerator of a rate is the number of times the event of interest, such as a dog bite, occurs over a given time period. The denominator is usually the average population size (such as the population of dogs) over the same time period.

$$\text{rate} = \frac{\text{number of events in a specified time period}}{\text{average population during the time period}}$$

The figure is usually multiplied by a convenient number to convert it from a fraction into a whole number. So, for example, if multiplied by 1000 it would then be the number of events per 1000 population for the specified time period. Try comparing the rate of bites from collies and Staffordshire bull terriers in the town of Barking (Exercise 2.2).

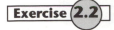

Here are some figures from the hypothetical town of Barking. In Barking in 1993, 20 people were bitten by Staffordshire bull terriers and 15 people were bitten by collies. Barking has a dog registration scheme and, assuming that all dogs are registered, it is known that in 1993 the average population of Staffordshire bull terriers in Barking was 200, and of collies was 150. Two dog owners are having a fierce debate over which breed is more likely to bite people. Assuming that each breed of dog spends the same amount of time around people, settle the dispute by calculating biting rates for each breed in 1993.

You should have found that the biting rates for collies and Staffordshire bull terriers were the same, i.e. 10 bites per 100 dogs per year.

What are incidence and prevalence?

You are likely to hear and read more about two types of rate than any others. They are called incidence and prevalence. These terms are used to refer to rates that measure the frequency of a disease or health condition in a population. The aim of this section is to explain to you what each term means, and how they differ. First work through Exercise 2.3.

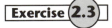

A nursing home has 100 residents. On the first day in January, 10 residents had a cold. Over the month of January, another 18 residents developed a cold. Assuming that the number of residents did not change over January, answer the following questions.

What proportion of the residents had a cold on the first day of January?

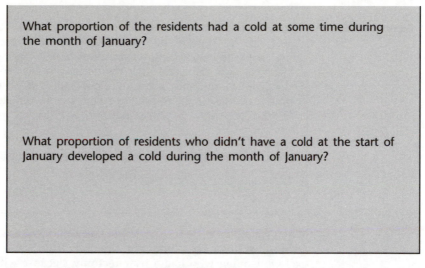

What proportion of the residents had a cold at some time during the month of January?

What proportion of residents who didn't have a cold at the start of January developed a cold during the month of January?

Exercise 2.3 may seem a little simple. It is supposed to! Many people find incidence and prevalence difficult concepts. In fact they are not, and you have just calculated the prevalence and incidence of the common cold among the hypothetical nursing home residents in the month of January.

Prevalence refers to *all* (prevAlence) people in a population with the disease or condition at a given point in time or over a given period of time. The general formula for calculating prevalence is:

$$\text{prevalence} = \frac{\text{total number of cases in a specified time period}}{\text{total population in the time period}}$$

Point prevalence refers to the proportion of people in a population with a disease or condition at one point in time. The point prevalence of the common cold among the nursing home residents in Exercise 2.3 on the first day of January was 10 per cent (10/100). *Period prevalence* is the proportion of people in a population known to have or have had a disease or condition at any time during a specified time period. The period prevalence for the month of January of the common cold among the nursing home residents in Exercise 2.3 was 28 per cent (28/100).

Incidence differs from prevalence in that it refers only to *new* (iNcidence) cases of a disease or condition that develop in a population over a specified period of time. The general formula for incidence is:

$$\text{incidence} = \frac{\text{number of new cases in specified time period}}{\text{population at risk in this time period}}$$

The 'population at risk' is an important concept. It refers to all people who *could* become new cases. In Exercise 2.3, ten of the nursing home residents already had a cold at the start of January and so could not become a new case over that month. Hence, 90 residents were 'at risk' of developing a cold for the first time during the month of January, and 18 did, giving an incidence of 20 per cent.

To consider the concept of 'population at risk' in more detail, work through Exercise 2.4.

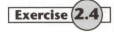

You are interested in the incidence of cancer of the uterus in your area. You find out the number of new cases over the past year from the cancer registry. This gives the numerator for calculating the incidence. The denominator is the population 'at risk'. Imagine you start with the number of the total population of your area for the past year. Make a list of everyone who should be excluded from this to leave you with the true population 'at risk'.

When calculating the incidence of cancer of the uterus you would clearly want to exclude men from the denominator. You would also want to exclude women who had a hysterectomy, because without a uterus they can no longer be at risk. You would also want to exclude women who had already had cancer of the uterus diagnosed before the specified time period, and who therefore could not become a new case. In practice you might find it difficult to define the size of the population at risk accurately. In your area the number of women should be known with reasonable accuracy (we hope), but information on the number of women with hysterectomies, for example, might be harder to find. When working through Exercise 2.4 you may also have been struck by the fact that it will often make sense to define the population at risk when calculating prevalence. For example, giving the prevalence of cancer of the uterus for the total population (men and women) would not make much sense because men cannot get it.

What is the relationship between incidence and prevalence?

The relationship between incidence and prevalence is summarized in the 'prevalence pot' (Figure 2.1). The amount of water in the pot represents how much of a particular disease there is in the population at any one time (the point prevalence). This is dependent on the rate of new cases of the disease entering the pot (the incidence) and the rate with which people with the disease leave the pot (recover or die), which is related to the duration of the disease. Notice that the prevalence pot in Figure 2.1 assumes that there is no migration of people with the disease into or out of the population.

A simple mathematical formula is often used to represent the relationship between incidence, prevalence and duration of a disease:

prevalence = incidence × average duration of the disease

This formula is only valid in the 'steady state' (when incidence and average duration can be assumed to have been constant over a long period

Incidence

Recovery
or death

Figure 2.1 The prevalence pot.

of time) and when the prevalence of the disease is low (i.e. 10 per cent
or less). None the less, it is a useful summary of the relationships between
incidence, prevalence and duration. Use the formula to solve the problems in Exercise 2.5.

Use the formula

   prevalence = incidence × average duration

to fill in empty boxes in the table below.

Condition	Incidence/ 100,000 population/ year	Point prevalence/ 100,000 population	Average duration (years)
Epilepsy	30		13
Brain tumours	20	65	
Multiple sclerosis		60	12

Which is the commonest (most prevalent) condition?

Which condition has the shortest duration?

Answers: epilepsy (390/100,000); brain tumours (3.25 years).

What are crude, specific and standardized rates?

Rates can be presented as crude, specific or standardized.

- *A crude rate* is that presented for an entire population.
- *A specific rate* is presented for a particular sub-group of a population. For example, age-specific rates are those presented for different age groups in a population; and sex-specific for men and women separately.
- *Standardized rates* are used to compare two or more populations with the effects of differences in age or other confounding variables removed. For example, one would expect a population of predominantly young adults to have a much lower crude death rate than a population of predominantly old adults. Techniques of standardization can be used to compare these two populations with the effects of the age differences removed.

The uses of crude, specific and standardized rates are illustrated in the following section on mortality rates.

Mortality rates

In Chapter 1 it was noted that routine information sources on morbidity are very limited, but that information on mortality tends to be much more readily available. For this reason, mortality rates are probably the single most important routinely available data source on the 'health' of populations. Familiarity with the use and interpretation of mortality rates is therefore very important.

Mortality rates are incidence rates – the incidence of death. In the rest of this section the uses and limitations of crude, specific and standardized mortality rates are illustrated by comparing the mortality experience of two real populations. One population consists of people resident in the City of Newcastle upon Tyne in the UK, and the other of people resident in Dar es Salaam in Tanzania.

Crude mortality rates

The crude mortality rate for a given year can be defined as:

$$\frac{\text{all deaths during the year}}{\text{population at the mid-year}}$$

Typically, mortality statistics which are routinely available are presented for a calender year (i.e. January to December), and usually the rate is multiplied by 1000 to give the number of deaths per 1000 population per year.

Now work through Exercise 2.6, but before you do so write down whether you think Newcastle or Dar es Salaam will have the higher crude mortality rate.

Crude mortality rates in Newcastle and Dar es Salaam

The table below shows the number of deaths and mid-year populations for the City of Newcastle upon Tyne in England in 1991 and an area in Dar es Salaam in Tanzania in 1992. Complete the table by calculating the crude death rates.

	Total deaths	Mid-year population	Death rate per 1000 population per year
Newcastle (1991)	3558	259,541	
Dar es Salaam (1992)	576	66,085	

Newcastle has the higher crude mortality rate. Is this the answer you expected?

Does the difference in crude mortality rates between Newcastle and Dar es Salaam mean that Dar es Salaam is the healthier population?

If your answer to the above question is 'no', what other reasons can you think of for differences in rates?

Sources of information: Office of Population Censuses and Surveys, London, for Newcastle upon Tyne; Adult Morbidity and Mortality Project, Dar es Salaam, Tanzania.

Exercise 2.6 shows that the crude mortality rate in Newcastle is over 50 per cent higher than the crude mortality rate in Dar es Salaam (i.e. 13.7 per 1000 per year versus 8.7 per 1000 per year). At first this result is surprising – a very poor city in Africa has a lower mortality than a much more prosperous city in England. The reason for it lies in the differences in age structure between the populations in Newcastle and Dar es Salaam. This is addressed in the next section.

Age- and category-specific mortality rates

An age-specific mortality rate is simply the mortality rate for a particular age group. For example, the rate per 1000 for persons aged 45–54 would be:

$$\frac{\text{number of deaths in people aged 45–54}}{\text{mid-year population of 45–54-year-olds}} \times 1000$$

The age-specific mortality rates for Newcastle and Dar es Salaam are shown in Table 2.1. Notice that in every age group the rates are higher in Dar es

Table 2.1 Death rates by age group for Newcastle upon Tyne and Dar es Salaam.

Age group (years)	Mortality rate (deaths per 1000 population per year)	
	Newcastle	*Dar es Salaam*
0–4	2.9	18.6
5–14	0.3	2.9
15–24	0.4	2.6
25–34	0.9	7.9
35–44	1.7	8.9
45–54	5.6	12.2
55–64	13.5	30.2
65–74	36.8	55.1
75–84	75.4	105.8
85+	173.8	174.9

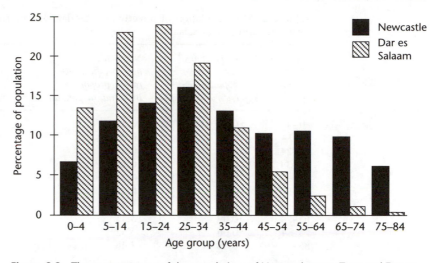

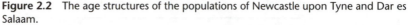

Figure 2.2 The age structures of the populations of Newcastle upon Tyne and Dar es Salaam.

Salaam. So there is an apparent paradox here: in every age group the rates are higher in Dar es Salaam yet the crude rate is higher in Newcastle. The reason for this is that the age structures of the two populations are very different. A much larger proportion of the population in Dar es Salaam consists of children and young adults. This is illustrated in Figure 2.2, which shows the distribution of the populations by broad age groups. You can see from Table 2.1 that although all the age-specific rates in Dar es Salaam are higher than in Newcastle, the death rates in children and young adults (e.g. below 35 years) in Dar es Salaam are still much lower than those in elderly people in Newcastle (e.g. 55 and above).

It is often informative to examine rates by other categories as well as age. For example, one could examine males and females separately. In fact, in both Newcastle and Dar es Salaam age-specific death rates are higher in men than in women: this is the picture in most populations around the world.

Cause-specific mortality rates refer to rates from specific causes of death, such as lung cancer or heart disease. For example, the rate of death from heart disease in men aged 45–54 for one year would be computed as:

$$\frac{\text{deaths from heart disease in men aged 45--54 in year}}{\text{number of men aged 45--54 at mid-year}} \times 1000$$

Let us sum this sub-section up. Crude mortality rates can be a very misleading way of comparing the mortality experience of different populations. Age is the single most important determinant of mortality and at the very least differences in age structure between the populations must be taken into account. Comparing age-specific death rates is one way to do this but can be cumbersome because it involves making many comparisons. However, single rates can be produced which have been adjusted for age differences between the populations. These are called age-adjusted or age-standardized rates.

Table 2.2 The calculation of directly age-standardized mortality rates for Newcastle and Dar es Salaam.

Age group (years)	Proportion of standard population in each age group	Newcastle age specific death rate × proportion in standard population	Dar es Salaam age specific death rate × proportion in standard population
0–4	0.07	0.21	1.30
5–14	0.12	0.03	0.35
15–24	0.14	0.05	0.36
25–34	0.16	0.15	1.26
35–44	0.14	0.24	1.24
45–54	0.12	0.68	1.47
55–64	0.1	1.35	3.02
65–74	0.09	3.31	4.96
75–84	0.06	4.52	6.35
85+	0.02	3.48	3.50
Total	1.00	14.02	23.81

The standard population used is the population of England and Wales in 1991. The age specific death rates used are those shown in Table 2.1.

The directly age-adjusted rate for Newcastle is 14.02 deaths per 1000 population per year, and for Dar es Salaam is 23.81 deaths per 1000 population per year.

How are age-standardized mortality rates produced?

Consider again the reason for the lower crude mortality rate in Dar es Salaam compared to Newcastle despite Dar es Salaam having higher age-specific rates. The reason was that in Dar es Salaam a much larger proportion of the population was made up of children and young adults than in Newcastle, and the death rates in the young people in Dar es Salaam were lower than in the older people in Newcastle. A crude mortality rate depends on the age-specific death rates *and* the proportion of the population in each of the age bands. This can be expressed a little more mathematically as follows:

crude mortality rate = sum of (each age specific mortality rate × proportion of the population in that age group)

There are two methods of age standardization, one called direct standardization and the other indirect standardization. The principle behind them both is the same.

In *direct standardization*, the proportions in each age group of a *standard population* are applied to the age-specific death rates of the populations being compared. This is illustrated for Newcastle and Dar es Salaam in Table 2.2. Look over this now.

The directly age-adjusted rate for Newcastle is 14.02 deaths per 1000 population per year, and for Dar es Salaam is 23.81. These can be shown as a ratio (one divided by the other), i.e. 23.81/14.02 = 1.7. This is called a *standardized rate ratio* and indicates that when differences in age structure are taken into account death rates in Dar es Salaam are 1.7 times those in Newcastle.

Indirect standardization follows the same principle as direct standardization, but with one very important difference. In indirect standardization a standard population is used to provide age-specific death rates, rather than providing the proportions of the population in different age groups. The age-specific death rates of the standard population are applied to the age groups of the population to which it is being compared. This gives the number of deaths in each group that would be expected if the population had the same age-specific death rates as the standard population. Using the number of 'expected' deaths and the actual number of deaths observed, a figure called the standardized mortality ratio (SMR) can be calculated. This is derived as follows:

$$\text{SMR} = \frac{\text{observed number of deaths}}{\text{expected number of deaths}}$$

The figure is traditionally multiplied by 100 to avoid cumbersome fractions. If the standard population and the population being compared had the same mortality experience, then the figure would be 100 because the expected and observed number of deaths would be equal. An SMR of greater than 100 means that the mortality in the population being compared is higher than in the standard, and less than 100 means that the mortality is lower. Table 2.3 demonstrates the calculation of the SMR for Newcastle using the age-specific death rates of England and Wales as standard.

In Table 2.3 the SMR for Newcastle is 114. This means that there were

Table 2.3 Calculation of the standardized-mortality ratio for Newcastle using the Population of England and Wales as the standard

Age groups	Age-specific death rates (per 1000 population) for England and Wales in 1991	Number of people (thousands) in Newcastle in 1991 by age group	Expected number of deaths in each age group
0–4	1.79	17.030	30
5–14	0.19	30.667	6
15–24	0.57	36.574	21
25–34	0.68	41.786	28
35–44	1.40	34.128	48
45–54	3.70	26.655	99
55–64	10.94	27.345	299
65–74	29.10	25.407	739
75–84	71.46	15.552	1111
85+	166.44	4.397	732
Total	–	259.541	3113

The table shows the calculation of the 'expected' number of deaths. The expected number of deaths for each age group is calculated by multiplying the number of people in Newcastle in that age group by the death rate for that age group in England and Wales.

$$\text{SMR} = \frac{\text{observed number of deaths}}{\text{expected number of deaths}} \times 100 = \frac{3558}{3113} \times 100 = 114$$

14 per cent more deaths in Newcastle in 1991 than would have occurred if it had the same age specific death rates as England and Wales in 1991.

What are the potential shortcomings of age-standardized mortality rates?

There are two potential shortcomings of using age-standardized mortality rates to consider. The first is general and the second refers specifically to indirectly standardized rates.

First, the use of a single figure (the age-adjusted rate) inevitably hides the detail of the age specific rates. Look again at the age-specific death rates for Newcastle and Dar es Salaam (Table 2.1). You will see that for most of the age groups the death rates in Dar es Salaam are well over twice as high as those in Newcastle. It is only in the older age groups that the difference between the death rates falls to less than two. So the standardized rate ratio of 1.7 seems to be a reasonable summary of the situation in the older age groups but a gross underestimate of the differences between Newcastle and Dar es Salaam in the younger age groups. The only way to give a clearer picture of the situation is to describe the actual age-specific death rates.

The interpretation of one indirectly standardized rate, or SMR, is straightforward. It is a comparison between the number of deaths expected if the study population had the same mortality experience as the standard population and the actual number of deaths in the study population. This comparison is made by weighting the age-specific death rates of the standard population by the age structure of the study population (i.e. the age-specific death rates are multiplied by the number of people in each age group in the study population). In Table 2.3 the age-specific death rates of England and Wales are weighted to the age structure of Newcastle. If the same process was carried out for Dar es Salaam, the rates would be weighted by the age structure of Dar es Salaam. Therefore, SMRs for Newcastle and Dar es Salaam would not be comparable because each SMR is based on a different age structure.

Having noted that SMRs should only be used to compare the standard population and one other population, you need to be warned that you will often see SMRs used to compare several populations. For example, in Britain SMRs are often used to compare the mortality experience in different health authorities. They have been used to compare the mortality experience in different social classes and in different immigrant groups. If the population age structures of the populations being compared are the same, then using SMRs is fine. If the population age structures are very different, as between Newcastle and Dar es Salaam, then using SMRs is likely to be very misleading. In most situations where SMRs are used the age structures of the populations being compared are probably not very different and the size of the error is therefore probably small. However, whenever you see SMRs being used to compare several populations, at least consider critically how valid the comparisons are likely to be.

The reason why the indirect method of standardization remains popular is that it has two practical advantages over the direct method. The first is that you don't need to know the age-specific death rates of the population being compared. All you need are the total number of deaths (the observed deaths) and the age structure (to be able to calculate the expected deaths). The second advantage of the indirect method is that it is subject to less random error than the direct method. This is because in the direct method the number of deaths used to calculate the age-specific death rates, particularly in the younger age groups, will often be very small and subject to quite marked variation from year to year and between populations. By using only the total number of deaths (the observed deaths), the indirect method is less subject to this type of error.

Summary

1 Write a short paragraph to explain to a colleague why rates are needed to make comparisons between populations. (Try making up a hypothetical example of your own to illustrate the point.)

2 Give the general formula for a rate.

3 Give the general formulas for incidence and prevalence.

4 Describe the relationship between incidence, prevalence and disease duration.

5 Define the following terms: (a) crude mortality rate; (b) age-specific mortality rate; (c) disease-specific mortality rate.

6 Describe the differences between direct and indirect age standardization.

7 Explain why the use of indirect standardization to compare more than two populations could in some circumstances be misleading.

CHAPTER 3

MEASURES OF RISK

What is relative risk?

What is a risk factor?

How do attributable and relative risk differ?

After working through this chapter you should be able to:

- define the term 'risk' as used in epidemiology;

- define relative risk;

- define and discuss what is meant by the term 'risk factor';

- define the terms 'attributable risk (exposed)' and 'attributable risk (population)';

- describe the main assumptions on which the use of attributable risk is based;

- discuss the relevance to public health of relative risk and attributable risk (exposed and population).

What is risk?

The word risk is used in everyday language. A risk is a hazard or a danger. To take a risk often means to undertake a dangerous activity. Rock climbing or hang gliding are often described as risky activities. To take a risk also implies chance: that there is a chance of an unpleasant or damaging event occurring. Another name for gambler is risk-taker.

Uses of the term risk from everyday language also help to capture the meaning of the term risk in epidemiology. It is about the chance or probability of events occurring. In epidemiology, as in everyday use, the events are usually undesirable, such as deaths or episodes of disease. However, a definition of risk that fits its use in epidemiology is simply this: *the probability that an event will occur*. The event need not be undesirable. It would make sense, for example, to refer to the risk (or probability) of cure of a disease by a particular drug.

Concepts of risk, or the probability of events, are central to epidemiology. This chapter aims to get across the basic concepts. All the examples in this chapter are based on a landmark study of modern epidemiology. It is a study of the relationship between smoking and cause of death in British doctors. The references for the papers on which these examples are based are given in Exercise 3.1 and you may find it helpful to look them up. Work now through this exercise.

Exercise 3.1

In October 1951, a short questionnaire was sent to the 59,600 men and women whose names were on the Medical Register of the United Kingdom. The questionnaire sought information on the smoking habits of the doctors. In all, 40,637 doctors (68 per cent) returned completed questionnaires. The number of doctors who had died, and their causes of death, were obtained – mainly from death certificates. Between 1 November 1951 and 31 October 1961 there were 4963 deaths. The death rates by smoking status for different causes of death are shown in the table below.

Cause of death	Deaths per 1000 persons per year			
	Total population	Non-smokers	All cigarette smokers	Cigarette smokers of ≥ 25 a day
All causes	14.05	12.06	16.32	19.67
Lung cancer	0.65	0.07	1.20	2.23
Coronary heart disease	3.99	3.31	4.57	4.97

1 What are the risks of death in the non-smokers and those smoking 25 or more cigarettes a day?

2 What is the risk of death from lung cancer in non-smokers, and the risk of death from lung cancer in those smoking 25 or more cigarettes a day?

3 Can you conclude from the figures in the table that smoking increases the risk of death?

Sources: R. Doll and A.B. Hill (1964) Mortality in relation to smoking: ten years' observation of British doctors. *British Medical Journal*, June, 1399–1410 and 1460–7.

The risks of death in Exercise 3.1 are in fact the death rates. The risk of death (from all causes) for non-smokers was 12.06 per 1000 persons per year, and for heavy smokers (25 or more cigarettes a day) was 19.67 per 1000 persons per year. If you wished, you could express these as percentages, i.e. 1.206 per cent per year and 1.967 per cent per year respectively. These figures represent the *absolute risk* of death among the non-smokers and heavy smokers in this study. Absolute risk is the same as incidence, in this case the incidence of death.

You may feel that the figures in the table provide strong evidence that smoking increases the risk (or incidence) of death. However, you may also feel that more information is required. At the very least you would want to know that the smokers and non-smokers were of similar ages – if the smokers were older then of course they would have higher death rates because the risk of death increases with age. In fact the figures in the table in Exercise 3.1 have been directly standardized (the technique is described in Chapter 2) to take account of differences in age and sex composition between the smokers and non-smokers. Of course, there may still be other differences between the smokers and non-smokers which account for the difference in the risk of death. The issue of deciding if a factor causes a disease is discussed in more detail in Chapter 5.

What is relative risk?

Relative risk is used to compare the incidence of a disease or condition between a group with a particular attribute or exposure to one without. It has the following form:

incidence in the group with attribute or exposure
───
incidence in group without attribute or exposure

This is illustrated in Exercise 3.2. Work through this now.

Taking the figures from the table in Exercise 3.1, the relative risk of all those smoking for death from lung cancer is:

$$\frac{1.20}{0.07} = 17.1$$

In plain English, this means that those smoking were 17 times more likely to die from lung cancer than non-smokers.

The relative risk of death from lung cancer for heavy smokers compared to non-smokers is:

$$\frac{2.23}{0.07} = 31.9$$

Now calculate the relative risks of death from coronary heart disease for smokers compared to non-smokers and heavy smokers compared to non-smokers.

Answers: 4.57/3.31 = 1.4; 4.97/3.31 = 1.5.

Relative risk is a measure of the strength of an association between an exposure or attribute and a disease. If the relative risk is 1 then the incidence in the two groups is the same. If it is greater than 1 then the attribute or exposure is associated with an increased incidence of the disease, and if less than one with a decreased incidence of the disease. For example, in the study of British doctors and smoking there was clearly a very strong association between mortality from lung cancer and smoking (relative risk 17.1), but a much less strong relationship between mortality from coronary heart disease and smoking (relative risk 1.4). An exposure which is positively associated with the occurrence of a disease, such as smoking is with lung cancer, is often called a risk factor for that disease.

What is the meaning of the term 'risk factor'?

The idea that different exposures, behaviours and personal attributes influence our risk of developing disease is a very old idea. The concept of 'risk factors', however, comes from modern epidemiology. It has its origins in some of the large prospective epidemiological studies (studies in which people are followed up over time to see who develops a disease and who does not) that were started after the Second World War. The study of the association of smoking behaviour of British doctors with causes of death is an example of this type of study. Another famous study which helped to establish the concept of 'risk factor' was started in a small town in New England in the United States of America. The town is called

Framingham and in the late 1940s male and female residents aged from 30 to 59 years underwent physical examinations, answered questions on personal behaviours, such as smoking, and had blood tests. Over 5000 who were free of coronary heart disease at the time of the examination were re-examined several times over many years to determine who developed coronary heart disease. In this way it was discovered that an increased risk of developing coronary heart disease was associated with smoking, high blood pressure, high serum cholesterol and other factors. These factors were called 'risk factors' for coronary heart disease.

The whole aim of identifying risk factors for a disease is to try to identify factors which may be causes of the disease and which if removed or modified would prevent the disease occurring. However, there is one very important message to take away from this section of the chapter. When an exposure or attribute is identified as a risk factor for a disease it simply means that *it is associated with an increased probability (risk) of the disease occurring*. It does not mean that the factor is a cause of the disease. For example, epidemiological studies have identified well over 200 risk factors for coronary heart disease. These include not having siestas, snoring, having English as a mother tongue and not eating mackerel. These factors have been associated with an increased risk of the disease but this does not indicate that they are causal. Changing the mother tongue in Britain to Italian is unlikely by itself to lower the levels of heart disease! Some authors have suggested that the term risk factor should be dropped and replaced by risk marker or risk indicator. These latter terms better convey the fact that it is a statistical association between the exposure or attribute and the outcome, and not necessarily a causal relationship. These issues are considered further in Chapter 5.

What is attributable risk?

Attributable risk is used to provide an assessment of how much of a disease is 'due to' an exposure and so how much *might* be prevented if an exposure is removed.

Below, definitions of two types of attributable risk are given. The first is for how much a disease among the *exposed* is 'due to' the exposure. The second is how much of the disease among the *total population* is 'due to' the exposure.

* *Attributable risk (exposed)* is the rate of a disease or condition amongst exposed individuals that can be attributed to the exposure.
* *Attributable risk (population)* is the rate of a disease or condition among the total population which can be attributed to the exposure.

The general formulas for calculating attributable risk (exposed) and attributable risk (population) are as follows.

attributable risk (exposed) = incidence among the exposed
                              − incidence among non-exposed

attributable risk (population) = incidence among total population
                              − incidence among non-exposed

These are often presented as proportions. For example, the percentage of cases of a disease in a population that are attributable to an exposure is:

$$\frac{\text{incidence among total population} - \text{incidence among non-exposed}}{\text{incidence among total population}} \times 100$$

By working through Exercise 3.3 you will get a better idea of how attributable risk is calculated and what it means.

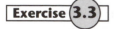

Look through the calculations of attributable risk (exposed) and attributable risk (population) for smoking and lung cancer. The figures are taken from the table in Exercise 3.1.

attributable risk (exposed) = 1.20 − 0.07
                            = 1.13 per 1000 persons per year

This can be interpreted as meaning that out of the 1.2 deaths from lung cancer per 1000 persons per year among the smokers, 1.13 were due to smoking. This can be expressed as a proportion, i.e.

$$\frac{1.20 - 0.07}{1.20} \times 100 = 94 \text{ per cent}$$

This can be interpreted as meaning that 94 per cent of the deaths from lung cancer among the smokers were due to smoking.

attributable risk (population) = 0.65 − 0.07
                              = 0.58 per 1000 persons per year

This can be interpreted as meaning that in the total population, 0.58 per 1000 deaths per year from lung cancer were due to smoking, or put as a proportion (0.58/0.65 x 100), 89 per cent of the lung cancer deaths in the total population were due to smoking.

Using the figures in the table in Exercise 3.1, carry out the same calculations for deaths from coronary heart disease.

Answers: attributable risk (exposed) = 1.26/1000 per year = 28 per cent; attributable risk (population) = 0.68/1000 per year = 17 per cent.

How should attributable risk be interpreted?

The simplest interpretation of attributable risk is that it represents the amount of the occurrence of a disease which is due to a particular exposure. So, for example, in the study of smoking among British doctors, smoking 'caused' 0.58 deaths from lung cancer per 1000 population per year, representing 89 per cent of all deaths from lung cancer (see Exercise 3.3). This interpretation, however, depends on two assumptions. The first is that the exposure (in this case smoking) causes the disease (lung cancer). The second is that other causes of the disease are equally distributed among the exposed (smokers) and unexposed (non-smokers).

A further interpretation that is usually placed apon attributable risk is that it represents the amount of a disease that could be prevented if the exposure were removed. This interpretation is based on a further assumption: that the rate of the disease in the exposed group will return to that in the non-exposed if the exposure is removed. How good this assumption is will depend on the exposure and disease. In the study of British doctors, for example, the death rates from lung cancer in those who had given up smoking did fall, but only in those who had given up smoking for around 20 years did the death rates approach those of non-smokers.

Let us sum up this section. Attributable risk is usually interpreted as providing an estimate of how much of a disease could be prevented if a particular exposure were removed. This interpretation is based on three assumptions: that the exposure causes the disease; that other factors causing the disease are equally distributed between the exposed and non-exposed groups; and that the rates of disease in the exposed group would fall to the rates in the non-exposed when the exposure were removed. Because of these assumptions attributable risk is best regarded as providing an assessment of the *maximum possible benefit* of removing the exposure.

What is the relevance to public health of relative risk and attributable risk?

Relative risk and attributable risk provide two very different types of information. Relative risk is a measure of the strength of the association between an exposure and a disease. It is used to help assess whether or not an exposure is one of the causes of a disease. The strength of the association and whether or not there is a 'dose–response' relationship between the occurrence of the disease and the exposure are two factors often used to assess if the exposure is likely to be causal. The strong association between smoking and lung cancer and the fact that the more cigarettes smoked the stronger the association (e.g. see Exercise 3.2: the relative risk for heavy smokers was 31.9 and for all smokers 17.1) are two factors which, together with others, have led to the conclusion that smoking is a cause of lung cancer.

The attributable risk (population) provides an estimate of the benefit that might be expected within the total population if exposure to a given factor is removed. Thus attributable risk (population) is useful to guide preventive health measures aimed at improving the health of a population. The potential benefits of removing different exposures can be assessed using attributable risk. This can be useful in helping to decide which exposures it is worth trying to prevent.

Finally, it is worth appreciating that the magnitude of the relative risk does not indicate the magnitude of the attributable risk. You can see this by looking again at Exercise 3.3. Both the attributable risk (exposed) and attributable risk (population) are higher for smoking and coronary heart disease than they are for smoking and lung cancer. This implies that if smoking were prevented in this population more deaths would be prevented from coronary heart disease than from lung cancer. This is simply due to the fact that coronary heart disease is a much commoner cause of death than lung cancer. Look again at the table in Exercise 3.1. The death rate in the total population from coronary heart disease was 3.99/1000 compared to 0.65/1000 for lung cancer. Seventeen per cent (the proportion of coronary heart disease deaths in the total population 'due to' smoking) of 3.99 is bigger than 89 per cent (the proportion of lung cancer deaths in the total population 'due to' smoking) of 0.65.

Summary

1 Define what is meant by the term 'risk' as used in epidemiology.

2 Give the general formula for relative risk.

3 A lay person has read of 200 'risk factors' for coronary heart disease. He or she is confused and worried about what it all means. Write a short paragraph to reassure him or her and explain what a 'risk factor' is.

4 Give the general formulas for attributable risk (exposed) and attributable risk (population).

5 Attributable risk is often interpreted as giving the amount of a disease that would be prevented if the exposure were removed. What are the assumptions on which this interpretation is based?

6 Write a short paragraph contrasting the different uses in public health of relative risk and attributable risk.

CHAPTER 4

EPIDEMIOLOGICAL STUDY DESIGNS

What types of epidemiological study are there?

Which study designs are used for identifying the amount of a disease or health condition?

Which study designs are used for identifying possible causes of a disease or health condition?

After working through this chapter you should be able to:

• provide a simple classification of the different types of study;

• describe and give examples of the main uses of each type of epidemiological study;

• discuss the strengths and weaknesses of the different types of epidemiological study designs.

What types of epidemiological study are there?

There is no single agreed classification of epidemiological studies, and in your reading you are likely to come across different terms for the same type of study. One approach to their classification is to consider their role within public health. Public health can be defined as 'one of the efforts organized by society to protect, promote and restore the people's health'. This broad definition includes finding out what the main health problems are and what the causes of the health problems are, and planning ways of preventing the health problems and of treating and caring for people with them. Epidemiology provides information which is essential (but by

Table 4.1 A classification of the main types of epidemiological studies

Main category	Types within category
Descriptive studies	Descriptions based on data sources already available Cross-sectional (prevalence) studies
Analytical studies	Ecological Cross-sectional Case–control Cohort
Intervention studies	Clinical trial Community trial

itself not enough) to guide and monitor public health activity. Broadly, epidemiological studies can provide information on three areas:

- on the distribution and frequency of diseases, and on the frequency and distribution of known and possible causes of diseases in populations – such studies are usually called *descriptive*;
- on the strength of associations between diseases and other factors (such as smoking, diet or socio-economic status), with particular emphasis on whether such associations are causal – such studies are usually called *analytical*;
- on whether interventions aimed at preventing a disease or improving its outcome actually do so – such studies are usually called *intervention* studies.

Within these three broad categories several types of study can be identified. These are summarized in Table 4.1.

What are descriptive studies used for and what types are there?

Descriptive studies are used to provide information on the frequency of diseases and their known and possible causes by person, place and time. Such information is crucial to guide the planning of health services and may also provide important clues to the causes of a disease. Some of the factors to consider under the headings of person, place and time are outlined below.

- *Person*: e.g. for a certain disease how old are the people who get it, what sex are they, what is their socio-economic status, what is their occupation, what is their ethnic group, what are their lifestyles like, such as smoking and diet, and so on?
- *Place*: e.g. is the occurrence of the disease more frequent in some geographical areas than others, such as between countries, areas within countries or areas within cities; do members of an ethnic group who have a low rate of the disease in one area also have a low rate when members of that ethnic group move to another area; and so on?

• *Time*: e.g. has the frequency of the disease changed over long periods of time, such as several years; does the frequency of the disease vary throughout the year and so on?

Many descriptive studies can be carried out using the type of routine information described in Chapter 1. Exercise 4.1 is based on routinely collected mortality data and shows death rates from coronary heart disease in men and women in England over a five-year period. Look at this now.

Exercise 4.1

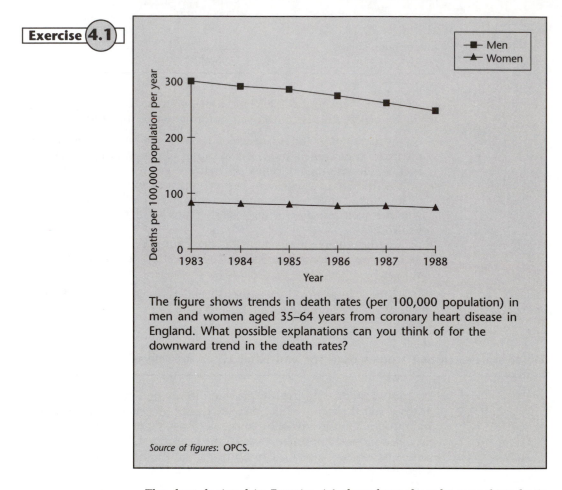

The figure shows trends in death rates (per 100,000 population) in men and women aged 35–64 years from coronary heart disease in England. What possible explanations can you think of for the downward trend in the death rates?

Source of figures: OPCS.

The data depicted in Exercise 4.1 show how thought provoking basic descriptive data can be. First, there is the very big difference in death rates in coronary heart disease between men and women. It is also possible using routine data to plot death rates by such factors as geographical area and social class. This would show, for example, that death rates from coronary heart disease are higher in the north of England than in the south, and also tend to be higher in lower socio-economic groups. Second, the downward trends are intriguing. Reasons for these are not clear, although similar trends in other countries have been associated with changes in the levels of coronary heart disease risk factors such as cholesterol levels and smoking.

As discussed in Chapter 1, routinely available data tend to be very limited, especially for looking at morbidity rather than mortality. Determining the frequency of a particular disease often requires a special study, the most common type being what is called a cross-sectional or prevalence survey. In a *cross-sectional* survey the health status of individuals, and any other factors of interest, are measured at one point in time. The most important use of cross-sectional surveys is to find the proportion of people within a population group who have a particular disease (or any other condition) of interest. Therefore, another commonly applied name for cross-sectional surveys is *prevalence* surveys. Knowledge of the prevalence of conditions is essential to be able to plan health services to treat those conditions.

Prevalence surveys may also be used to examine associations between a disease and possible causes of the disease. Thus, depending on how they are analysed and used, cross-sectional studies can be classified with either descriptive or analytical studies. The use of cross-sectional studies for examining associations between diseases and possible causes is discussed in the next section.

What are analytical studies used for and what types are there?

Analytical studies are used to identify associations between a disease and possible causes of the disease. Types of study which are used for this are ecological, cross-sectional, cohort and case–control studies.

In an *ecological study*, data are collected on whole groups or populations of people rather than on individuals. Usually routinely collected data on disease rates are compared with data on the possible causes of the disease within the same populations or groups. Exercise 4.2 is based on some results from a famous study in the United States, which examined the relationship between the prevalence of dental caries within a population and the concentration of fluoride in the water supply. Have a look at this exercise now.

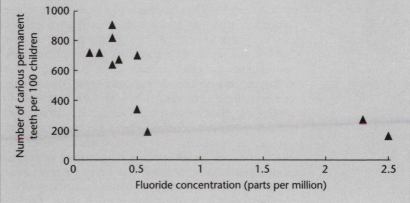

The figure shows the relationship between the number of dental caries per 100 children (aged 12–14 years) and the concentration of fluoride in the water supply for 11 towns in the United States. What is the nature of the relationship? What explanations can you think of for this relationship?

Source of figures: D. Trendley (1938) Endemic fluorosis and its relation to dental caries. *Public Health Reports*, 53(33), 1443–52.

The main advantage of ecological studies is that they tend to be conducted using routinely collected data and therefore they can usually be done quickly and inexpensively. The study in Exercise 4.2 suggested that towns with higher fluoride levels in the water have lower levels of caries. The major disadvantage of ecological studies is that they are based on groups of people and not on individuals. It is possible that there are many differences between the towns in Exercise 4.2 apart from fluoride level which might account for the different levels of caries: an association found at the group level may not exist at the individual level, or conversely there may be no association found at the group level when in fact one does exist at the individual level. In either case, the wrong conclusion would be drawn from the ecological study. This type of misleading result is called an 'ecological fallacy'. Therefore, ecological studies are best seen as useful means of generating hypotheses on the possible causes of diseases, hypotheses which can be tested in more detailed studies, which, of course, was the case with the hypothesis that fluoride helps protect against tooth decay.

As was discussed in the previous section, *cross-sectional studies* or *prevalence surveys* may be used to identify associations between diseases and possible causes. The drawback of a prevalence survey in looking for associations is that the study is only at one point in time. For example, a cross-sectional study into the prevalence of diabetes in adults may find that people with diabetes tend to be more obese than people without diabetes. Whether obesity leads to diabetes or whether diabetes leads to obesity cannot be determined from this type of study. Given such an observation, one might hypothesize that obesity increases the risk of developing diabetes and then undertake more appropriate studies to see if the hypothesis is correct. There are, however, some situations in which one can be confident that the risk marker preceded the onset of the disease. For example, genetically determined factors such as sex and blood group clearly must precede the onset of any disease developed in later life, but even in this situation the fact that there is an association does not mean that it is the cause of the disease. Assessing whether an association is likely to be causal is covered in Chapter 5. Looking for associations within cross-sectional studies is best seen as an aid to generating ideas on the causes of a disease: if associations are found this can provide the basis for more detailed work to try to determine if such associations are causal.

Case–control studies compare people with the disease of interest (cases) to people without the disease (controls) and look for differences in past exposure to possible causes of the disease. Exercise 4.3 is based on a hypothetical food poisoning outbreak. Case–control studies are very commonly used in this situation to try to identify which food was responsible. Look at this now.

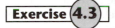

The table below shows some hypothetical results from an investigation of a food poisoning outbreak at a wedding reception. There were 100 guests and 25 reported vomiting within 24 hours of attending the reception. A list was made of all the foods available at the reception and all the guests were asked which they had eaten. The table shows the results for the salmon mousse.

	Ate salmon mousse	
Food poisoning	Yes	No
Yes	20	5
No	15	60

The strength of association between having food poisoning and eating the salmon mousse is calculated as the 'odds ratio' (OR for short), which is the chance of eating the mousse (exposure) among those with food poisoning (20/5) divided by the chance of exposure in those without food poisoning (15/60), which works out at 16. Thus, in this hypothetical example those with food poisoning were 16 times more likely to report eating salmon mousse than those without.

Does this mean that salmon mousse was the source of the food poisoning?

If it does, what explanation might there be for the five cases who said they didn't eat mousse, and the 15 who didn't report vomiting who said they did eat the mousse?

The figures in Exercise 4.3 provide strong evidence that the salmon mousse was the source of the food poisoning, but there are other possible explanations. For example, people who ate the mousse may have been more likely to eat another dish as well; perhaps it was served with a sauce which was the cause of the food poisoning. This might then explain why not all the cases reported eating mousse; perhaps they tried the sauce only. However, also note in Exercise 4.3 that food poisoning was simply referred to as people who reported vomiting, and not all the vomiting may have been due to food poisoning. Conversely, the 15 people who ate the mousse but didn't vomit may have had other symptoms of food poisoning or may not have eaten enough to become ill.

In case–control studies the strength of the association between the disease and an exposure is measured by calculating the odds ratio. This is illustrated in Exercise 4.3. As discussed in Chapter 3, relative risk provides the most direct measure of an association between a disease and possible causes. Relative risk is the incidence of the disease in individuals exposed to a potential cause divided by the incidence of the disease in the unexposed. Case–control studies start with people with and without the disease of interest and do not therefore measure disease incidence. However, it can be shown that if certain conditions are met, the odds ratio found in a case–control study is a valid and close estimate of relative risk. These conditions are not discussed in detail here, but include that the cases of the disease are newly diagnosed (that they are what are called 'incident cases'), that prevalent cases are not included in the control group and that the selection of cases and controls is independent of exposure status. Most case–control studies are designed to meet these conditions, and it is a big bonus of the case–control study design that it is able to provide a valid estimate of relative risk.

In mischievous moments some commentators have suggested that the results from case–control studies must always be taken with a pinch of salt. This is because case–control studies are particularly prone to some types of bias. Bias, which can be defined as systematic error or deviation of results or inferences from the truth, is discussed in more detail in the next chapter. Two types of bias to which case–control studies are particularly prone are touched on here. The first is information bias, i.e. bias arising from the way information is collected in the study. Case–control studies are particularly prone to one type of information bias, known as recall bias. Recall bias refers to differences between cases and controls in the completeness of recall to memory of past events or experiences. This may arise because cases try harder to remember past events than controls – the presence of a serious disease can certainly focus the mind, and lead to the subjects searching their memory for events which may provide some explanation as to why they developed the disease. Recall bias may also arise because the person interviewing the cases and controls questions the cases more thoroughly than the controls. The interviewer may have his or her own views about the causes of the disease and so tend to press the cases a little harder on these issues than the controls. Another form of bias to which case–control studies are particularly prone arises from the selection and comparison of cases and controls. It needs to be crystal clear what population the cases in the study represent. The controls should be representative of the population from which the cases came, which is generally taken to mean that had the controls developed the disease they would have been selected as cases in the study.

Case–control studies have several advantages. They are comparatively cheap and quick to conduct, giving an answer as to the possible causes of a disease within a relatively short period of time. Because the investigator starts with people with a given disease, rather than following people up to see who will develop the disease as in cohort studies (described below), they are good for investigating the causes of rare diseases. In addition, a whole range of possible causes for a single disease can be investigated within one study.

In a *cohort study*, two or more groups of people who are free of the disease of interest but who differ according to exposure to a potential cause or causes are followed up over time to compare the incidence of the disease in each group. (The term *cohort* simply refers to any designated group of people who are followed up over a period of time.) The study of doctors and smoking described in Exercise 3.1 is an example of a cohort study. Look back briefly over this example now. This study was set up after a case–control study comparing patients with lung cancer to patients with other conditions (mainly patients with cancers at other sites) suggested the link between smoking and lung cancer. It is quite common for a cohort study to be set up to determine if associations found in a case–control study are also found in a cohort study. If the associations are found in both types of study, this strengthens the evidence that the associations are real. Whether or not the associations are *causal* is a separate question and addressed in detail in the next chapter.

In cohort studies the strength of the association between the disease (or other outcome of interest) and possible cause of the disease is measured by comparing the incidence of the disease in those exposed to the possible cause and the incidence of the disease in those not exposed.

Because in cohort studies exposures to potential causes of a disease are defined before the disease develops, they are less prone to information bias than case–control studies. In addition, cohort studies directly measure the relative risks associated with different exposures. For these reasons in particular, the information derived from cohort studies is often given greater weight than information derived from case–control studies. Cohort studies are also good for looking at the effects of rare exposures, because individuals can be selected on the basis of exposure at the start of the study. A cohort study can also examine multiple possible outcomes from a single exposure.

However, cohort studies do have several drawbacks. They are a very inefficient way of looking for the potential causes of rare diseases. For example in a disease with an incidence of 1 per 100,000 per year, around one million individuals would need to be followed up for ten years to collect 100 cases. It is important that as many as possible of the individuals who originally entered the study are followed up. Keeping track of individuals is often an expensive and time consuming process, but if losses to follow-up are large, the findings may be quite misleading (because those lost to follow-up may differ from the rest). Finally, cohort studies (unless

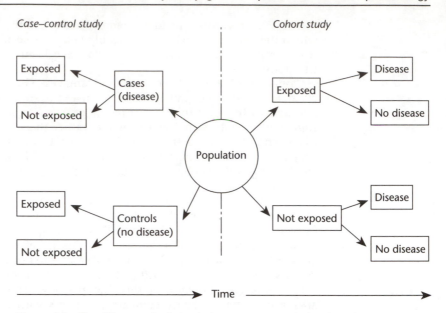

Case–control study

Cohort study

Figure 4.1 The differences in design between a case–control and a cohort study.

a 'historical cohort study', described below) do not give quick answers. Often follow-up over several years is required to collect enough cases of the disease to allow meaningful analysis.

Cohort and case–control studies can be regarded as investigating the potential causes of a disease from opposite directions. In a cohort study one starts with people free from the disease but exposed to different potential causes of the disease. In a case–control study one starts with people with and without the disease and then assesses their past exposure to potential causes of the disease. The relationship between cohort and case–control studies is illustrated in Figure 4.1. Because case–control studies look back in time they are often called *retrospective studies*; and because cohort studies normally follow people up over time they are often called *prospective studies*. However, these names can be confusing and are best avoided. For example, it is possible to have a 'retrospective' or 'historical' cohort study, in which the exposure status of individuals is identified from previous medical records and the individuals are then examined to determine their current health status. The key point is not whether the investigation is retrospective or prospective but whether the starting point was to identify individuals with or without a particular disease (case–control study) or to identify individuals according to their exposure status (cohort study).

A neat and increasingly used study design which combines some of the advantages of the cohort and case–control approaches is called the *nested case–control study*. In this design, data on exposure status are collected on a cohort of individuals, and thus following the cohort study approach, exposure status is defined prior to disease onset. This cohort is followed up and people who develop the disease of interest are identified.

Rather than these being compared with *all* the individuals who do not develop the disease, controls, perhaps two or three per case, are selected from the cohort and the study is then carried out like a case–control study. This makes the study much cheaper and quicker to carry out. This is particularly useful if the measurements of the exposure are expensive. For example, blood samples on every member of the cohort could be taken at the outset of the study and stored in a freezer. Only samples of people who develop the disease (cases) and those chosen as controls will then be analysed.

What are intervention studies used for and what types are there?

The key difference between analytical and intervention studies is this: in an analytical study the investigator simply observes the exposure status of individuals; in an intervention study the investigator intervenes to change the exposure status of individuals to determine what happens when this is done. In short, the investigator is conducting an experiment and for this reason another name for intervention studies is 'experimental studies'.

There are two broad types of intervention study: clinical trials and community trials. These study types are analogous to two types of analytical studies: cohort and ecological studies respectively. In a clinical trial the unit of study is the individual and the investigator intervenes to change the exposure status of individuals, and in community trials the unit of study is the group or population and the investigator intervenes to change the exposure status of whole groups or populations of people.

In a *clinical trial* one group of individuals receive an intervention and are compared to another group who do not receive the intervention. Clinical trials are often divided into two types: therapeutic or secondary prevention trials, and preventive or primary prevention trials. Therapeutic trials are conducted among patients with a particular disease to determine the ability of an intervention (such as a drug, changes in diet or psychological counselling) to diminish symptoms, prevent recurrence or decrease the risk of death from that disease. A preventive trial is used to evaluate whether an intervention reduces the risk of developing a disease among those who are free from it when they enter the trial.

As in all epidemiological studies, bias is a potential problem, and one which must be guarded against. The gold standard design for clinical trials, i.e. that which is least prone to bias, is the *randomized double blind* controlled trial.

Randomized refers to the fact that subjects are assigned to the intervention or control group at random and that neither the investigator nor the subject has any say in who goes into which group. This avoids the potential bias of the investigator choosing subjects he or she feels would be most likely to benefit from the intervention for the intervention group, and a similar possible bias if the choice were left up to the subjects. Clearly, for this to work subjects must agree to take part in the study before randomization – if their agreement to participate is dependent upon which group they are randomized to, this could also produce quite different types of subjects in the intervention and control groups. It is sometimes argued that surely it would be better for the investigator to decide who goes into the intervention and control groups because he or she could then make sure that the two groups are comparable rather than leaving it to chance. For example, the investigator could try to ensure that the groups were comparable in such things as the age of the subjects, their sex, risk behaviours such as smoking, severity of disease and so on. There are at least two reasons why randomization is still preferable. First, there may be unknown factors which could influence the outcome. Randomization ensures, within the limits of chance, that any such factors are evenly distributed between the intervention and control groups. Second, however hard the investigators try to produce two similar groups, it remains possible that they will be biased in their allocation of subjects, perhaps in ways of which they are not really aware.

Double blind refers to the fact that neither the investigator nor the subject knows whether he or she is in the intervention group. Clearly, this is not always possible for practical reasons. It is most obviously possible when the intervention is a drug. In this situation, the intervention group can receive a tablet which contains the drug and the control group receive an identical looking tablet which does not. With the correct organizational arrangements, neither the subjects nor the investigators need know who is receiving the intervention and who is not. Only at the end of the study would the 'code' be broken and the results analysed according to who had been taking the drug and who had not. The reason for going to all this trouble is to avoid the bias that may be introduced by the subjects' or the investigators' expectations about whether or not the drug works. Thus, for example, subjects who knew they were taking the tablet without the drug would not expect any benefit, whereas subjects taking the tablet with the drug would. Because of this expectation, subjects taking the tablet with the drug may feel and report benefits even if the drug is of no use at all. This effect is known as the placebo effect.

In a *community trial*, the units of study are communities rather than individuals. This is particularly appropriate for diseases that have their origins in social, cultural or environmental conditions, where it makes sense to try to change these conditions on a community-wide basis rather than an individual basis. For example, a community trial aimed at changing diet might include widespread information campaigns using the local media, as well as measures to increase the availability of healthy foods. There are two main limitations to community trials. First, it is usually only possible for practical reasons to include a small number of communities, making random allocation less likely to be successful in achieving comparable groups. Thus, usually non-random allocation is used to try to ensure that the groups are comparable. The second limitation is that it is very difficult to isolate the control from the intervention communities. The control communities are almost bound to be aware of what is going on in the intervention community and may therefore also change.

Summary

Use the following questions to write your own summary.

1 Distinguish between what is meant by the terms descriptive, analytical and intervention when referring to types of epidemiological study.

2 Outline the design of studies you would use to do the following:

- evaluate whether a new drug is effective in treating a condition;

- examine the cause of death by age, sex and area of residence for people living in England last year;

- measure the amount of diabetes in a population;

- examine whether people exposed to an unusual industrial chemical are at an increased risk of developing certain diseases;

- determine whether a mass media campaign to encourage people to change an aspect of their lifestyle is effective;

- identify possible causes of a rare disease.

CHAPTER 5

WEIGHING UP THE EVIDENCE FROM EPIDEMIOLOGICAL STUDIES

Why are bias, confounding and chance possible explanations for an association found in an epidemiological study?

How can bias be minimized?

How can confounding be addressed?

What is meant by 'statistical significance'?

How can you assess the causality of an association?

After working through this chapter, you should be able to:

• discuss the roles of bias, confounding and chance as possible explanations for associations found in a study;

• outline how bias, confounding and chance can be addressed in the design or analysis of a study;

• compare and contrast the concepts of association and causality.

Association and causation

One of the main uses of epidemiological studies is to identify associations between exposures and health outcomes. One way in which this is commonly done is to compute relative risk, which is the incidence of the health outcome in those exposed divided by the incidence of the health outcome in those not exposed. For example, the incidence of lung cancer in heavy cigarette smokers is around 20 times higher than in non-smokers.

This relative risk of 20 indicates a very strong association between cigarette smoking and lung cancer. It may seem tempting to conclude from this fact alone that cigarette smoking causes lung cancer. However, this conclusion cannot be reached so easily. Two questions must be addressed. First, it must be asked whether the association found between an exposure and an outcome in a study is real. There are many reasons why an association may be found in a study (for example, to do with how the study population was chosen and the data were collected), when in fact no association exists in the wider population. Second, if it seems likely that the association is real, the aphorism must be remembered: association does not mean causation. Assessing whether an association is likely to be causal is a judgement made in the light of all the available evidence, which includes evidence from disciplines other than epidemiology. The process of deciding whether an association is real and then whether it is likely to be causal is the subject of this chapter. However, before proceeding we must give some consideration to what is meant when we call something the 'cause' of a disease or other health state.

The subject of causality runs deep and remains the subject of much philosophical debate. A pragmatic approach to causality which fits the aims of public health is to refer to 'causes' of a disease as those factors which, if modified, whether singly or in combination, lead to a change in the incidence of the disease. Work now through Exercise 5.1.

What causes tuberculosis? Consider whether the following statements are true or false and give the reasons for your opinion.

1 Tuberculosis is caused by tuberculosis bacteria.

2 Tuberculosis is caused by poor housing, overcrowding, malnutrition and poverty.

3 Tuberculosis is caused by increased susceptibility to infection.

Without tuberculosis bacteria, tuberculosis (TB) cannot occur. They must be present. They are a *necessary cause*. However, exposure to tuberculosis bacteria alone is not *sufficient cause*. For example, someone who is healthy and well nourished is unlikely to develop TB after coming into contact with tuberculosis bacteria (of course, it will also depend on the level and length of exposure). Most causes that are of interest in the field of public health are not on their own sufficient to cause disease. They are components of sufficient causes. In the case of tuberculosis, we know of several *component causes* that contribute to a person developing the disease. Environmental factors, such as overcrowded/living conditions and malnutrition, are important. The susceptibility of the individual is important: an individual whose immune system is weakened by another disease is more susceptible to contract tuberculosis. Thus, poor living conditions, immunosuppression and tuberculosis bacteria are all component causes of TB, and together they may form *sufficient cause* (i.e. cause the disease).

To plan preventive action for health, it is not necessary always to identify all the components of a sufficient cause, because intervening at one component may be adequate to break the chain of events. In the case of tuberculosis, we know that death rates from the disease in England and Wales fell from almost 4000 per million people in 1840, to around 600 per million people in 1940, before any effective chemotherapy or vaccination was available. This decline seems to have been largely owing to improvements in nutrition and housing conditions. Around 1840, many people were affected by malnutrition and were living in overcrowded and damp houses. With the decline in the prevalence of these component causes, the incidence of TB declined because fewer people were exposed to sufficient cause. This example also illustrates that the strength of a causal risk factor is often dependent on the prevalence of other factors. For example, the risk of developing TB after exposure to the bacteria is higher in malnourished populations than well nourished ones.

Answering the question: 'is the association real?'

Epidemiological research is not a laboratory science; it is conducted with humans living within their environment. This is a strength and a weakness of epidemiology. The strength is the very fact that people are studied in their natural environment. The weakness is that the epidemiological researcher has limited control over many of the factors influencing the health of individuals. This means that the first step of any epidemiological study is to assess whether an observed association is real or whether there are alternative explanations for it. (The converse is also the case: no association may be found when in fact one exists.) To help to illustrate the process of making this assessment, we will refer to a well known study which examined the relationship between exposure to asbestos and deaths from lung cancer. In this study, the causes of death diagnosed at autopsy of men employed in an asbestos works over a 20-year period (1933–52) were reviewed. The researcher calculated how many deaths would have been expected in total and from different causes if the workers had the

Table 5.1 Causes of death among male asbestos workers compared with mortality experience of all men in England and Wales

Cause of death	Number of observed deaths	Number of deaths expected on England and Wales rates
Lung cancer	11	0.8
Neoplasm (other than lung cancer)	4	2.3
All causes	39	15.4

Source: adapted from R. Doll (1955) Mortality from lung cancer in asbestos workers. *British Medical Journal*, 12, 81–6.

same death rates as men in England and Wales over the same period of time. Some of the results from this study are shown in Table 5.1. While we work through this example, a framework will be followed which can be used to assess the nature of associations reported in any epidemiological study. This framework is illustrated in Figure 5.1. Look at this now before reading on.

Assessing the role of bias

Bias can be defined as any systematic error in an epidemiological study that results in an incorrect estimate of the association between an exposure and the occurrence of a disease. Bias can be divided into two broad types: selection bias and information bias.

- *Selection bias* refers to any systematic error that arises in identifying or recruiting the subjects to the study. This can occur in several ways. For example, the people who agree to take part in a study may be quite different from those who do not. Thus, those who agree to take part may not be representative of the population from which the sample was taken. This example of selection bias is called response bias.
- *Information bias* refers to systematic error which results from the way in which the data are collected. For example, in case–control studies (these are described in Chapter 4), data on exposure are usually collected retrospectively, often by interview. It is possible that people with the disease (cases) will report their history of exposure differently from those without, simply because the presence of the disease focuses the mind. This example of information bias is called recall bias, and may result in an association being found between an exposure and a disease when in fact none exists.

Look now at Exercise 5.2. This addresses some of the biases that were considered as possible explanations for the association between working with asbestos and death from lung cancer shown in Table 5.1.

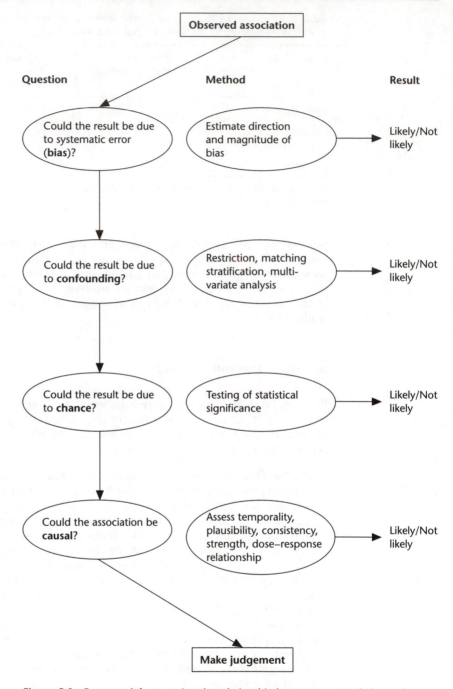

Figure 5.1 Framework for assessing the relationship between an association and an outcome.

Look at the results in Table 5.1 again. Consider the following suggested biases and write down your opinion on whether or not they could be responsible for the association between working with asbestos and lung cancer.

- Asbestos workers were more likely to be incorrectly diagnosed as suffering from lung cancer than men in England and Wales.

- Lung cancer was insufficiently diagnosed in the general population compared to asbestos workers.

- Pathologists were more likely to report lung cancer in autopsies on asbestos workers compared to autopsies in the general population.

Clearly the examples of potential bias given in Exercise 5.2 could all account for an apparent association between asbestos workers and lung cancer when none exists. Such potential biases were carefully considered by the author of the paper, who concluded that there was no evidence that such biases could account for the observed association.

Bias cannot be controlled for at the analysis stage of a study, but needs to be prevented and controlled through careful design of the study. The choice and recruitment of the study population, the methods of data collection and the sources of information about exposure and disease need to be carefully planned and executed to avoid bias.

Assessing the role of confounding

A second alternative explanation for an observed association is the mixing of effects by a third factor, which is associated with the exposure and independently with the risk of developing the disease. This is called confounding. Work through Exercise 5.3 before reading on.

Assume that all workers in the asbestos and lung cancer study were heavy smokers. Write down how you think this might have affected the results of the study.

If the proportion of smokers among the asbestos workers was much higher than the proportion of smokers in the general population, this could have accounted at least in part for the higher lung cancer rates among the workers. In 1955, when this study was published, smoking was not yet considered to be associated with lung cancer. Later studies in asbestos workers established that asbestos was associated with lung cancer independently from smoking, and found that smokers who worked with asbestos had an even higher risk of developing lung cancer than smokers who did not.

There are several methods to control for confounding in epidemiological studies. Some are applied when designing a study, others are used during the analysis of data. In an intervention study (described in Chapter 4), subjects can be randomized to the intervention and control groups. Randomization will ensure, within the limits of chance, that all potential confounding factors are evenly distributed between the intervention and control groups. There are, however, many situations where randomization cannot be applied. An alternative approach in the design of a study to control for confounding is to restrict our study sample to only those individuals that do not have a suspected or known confounding factor (restriction). For example, all smokers could have been excluded from a study of asbestos exposure and lung cancer. Disadvantages of restricting the sample include that the number who can be studied might become too small to give a meaningful result, and that those studied may be quite atypical of the general exposed population. An often better approach is to include all groups in the study, such as smokers and non-smokers, and then to look at those groups separately in the analysis, a procedure which is called stratification.

Another method of dealing with confounding is to look at subjects in matched pairs. In our asbestos–lung cancer example we could form pairs between smokers who worked in the asbestos industry and smokers who did not work in the asbestos industry, and similarly with non-smokers. We could match for other variables as well. For example, we might match pairs on the basis of age, sex and social class as well as smoking status. The disadvantage of this approach is that it can be very difficult, time consuming and therefore expensive. It can also present problems in finding enough people who can be matched.

Nowadays, with the power provided by personal computers, the most

Table 5.2 Causes of death among male asbestos workers compared with mortality experience of all men in England and Wales, plus p values for the difference between the observed and expected deaths

Cause of death	Number of observed deaths	Number of deaths expected on England and Wales rates	Probability (p)
Lung cancer	11	0.8	< 0.001
Neoplasm (other than lung cancer)	4	2.3	> 0.1
All causes	39	15.4	< 0.001

Source: adapted from R. Doll (1955) Mortality from lung cancer in asbestos workers. *British Medical Journal*, 12, 81–6.

common approach to control for confounding is to do so using statistical methods at the analysis stage of a study. There are statistical analysis techniques such as multivariate analysis which allow for the estimation of an association between an exposure and a disease while controlling for several confounding factors simultaneously.

Assessing the role of chance

The third alternative explanation for an observed association is that it has arisen by chance alone. Assessing the role of chance involves the use of a statistical approach known as hypothesis or significance testing. Space does not permit full justice to be done here to the process of significance testing and the assumptions on which it is based. Here the main steps in the process and the reasoning behind them are outlined. Table 5.2 contains the results shown in Table 5.1 but also contains an additional column showing the p values for the difference between the observed and expected values. How these were derived and how they are interpreted are summarized below.

Steps in testing statistical significance:

1 *State the research hypothesis.* In the case of asbestos exposure and lung cancer, the research hypothesis might be framed as 'asbestos exposure is associated with lung cancer'.
2 *Formulate the statistical hypothesis.* The statistical hypothesis translates the research hypothesis into a form to which statistical tests can be applied. This is done by formulating what is called the null hypothesis. The null hypothesis states that the results observed in a study are no different from what might have occurred by chance alone. In the example of the study into asbestos exposure and lung cancer, the null hypothesis would be that there is no difference in the death rate from lung cancer in asbestos workers and in the general population. The test of statistical

significance gives the probability of the observed results arising by chance. For example, a significance level with a p value of 0.1 indicates that, assuming the null hypothesis is correct, the probability of obtaining the result in the study, or a more extreme result, is 0.1 or 10 per cent. Put another way, simply by chance alone this result (or one more extreme) would be expected in 10 per cent of cases.

3 *Specify the rules to evaluate the null hypothesis.* It is common practice to specify a level of statistical significance against which to evaluate the null hypothesis. The most commonly used level of statistical significance is 5 per cent, also expressed as $p <$ (less than) 0.05. Thus, if the level is below 5 per cent it is standard practice to reject the null hypothesis and to assume that the observed results are unlikely to be due to chance; conversely, if the level is above 5 per cent it is standard practice to accept the null hypothesis and assume that the results may well be due to chance. The lower the value of p, the more we will be inclined to reject the null hypothesis.

4 *Carry out the analysis and interpret the statistics.* The final steps of the testing for statistical significance are to compute the tests (nowadays almost always done on computer) and to interpret the results. If you look at the p values in Table 5.2 you will see, for example, that the p value for lung cancer was less than 0.001, or 1 in 1000. This means that if the null hypothesis were true the results obtained would be expected by chance alone on fewer than 1 in 1000 occasions. Thus the explanation that the association between lung cancer and asbestos workers was due to chance (the null hypothesis) was rejected.

It cannot be emphasized too strongly that the cut-off point of 5 per cent for statistical significance, or any other cut-off point that may be used, is entirely arbitrary, and that the inflexible use of an arbitrary cut-off point often makes a nonsense of the interpretation of data. It is common in medical papers to see significance levels as different as 0.051 and 0.8 both simply described as 'non-significant'. However, clearly the probability of obtaining a result by chance alone of 5.1 per cent conveys a very different picture from a probability of 80 per cent. Another problem inherent in the interpretation of a p value results from the fact that it reflects both the magnitude of any difference between the groups being compared and the size of the sample. A small difference in a large sample or a large difference in a small sample can lead to similar p values. Today, many epidemiologists prefer to base statistical inference on what are called 'confidence intervals'. The confidence interval reports a range of values which have a specified probability of containing the true value. In Table 5.2, confidence intervals could be put on the size of the difference between the observed and the expected number of deaths. This would convey information on the likelihood of observing that difference by chance, but in addition it would convey information on where the true difference may lie.

Finally, it must be appreciated, but unfortunately it often is not, that statistical significance does not mean clinical importance. A small effect may be statistically significant if the size of the sample studied is large, but be of little clinical importance. Conversely, a large effect may fail to reach statistical significance if the sample size is small, but potentially be of great importance for health.

When does association mean causation?

Once we have established an association between an exposure and a disease (or other health outcome), and we have carefully considered and ruled out bias, confounding and chance as likely explanations, the next step is to make a judgement as to whether the association is likely to be causal. There is no watertight method of making such a judgement. Criteria have been suggested which taken together may strengthen or weaken the case that the association is causal. These include the following.

- *The strength of the association*: a strong association (e.g. with a large relative risk) is less likely to be owing to undetected biases than to a weak association. But a weak association could still be causal.
- *Consistency*: finding the same association in different studies, on different populations under different circumstances. But some causes may only operate in specific circumstances.
- *Temporality*: the cause must precede the effect in time. No 'buts' for this criterion.
- *Dose–response relationship*: it is suggested that a causal relationship is likely to show a dose–response relationship; that is, the greater the exposure the greater the chance of the disease. This is certainly the case for cigarette smoking and lung cancer. But for some causes any exposure may be enough, and conversely a dose–response relationship could still be due to confounding.
- *Biological plausibility*: are there known biological mechanisms by which the exposure could cause the disease? But clearly lack of an obvious mechanism does not mean it is not causal.
- *Experimental evidence*: may be available from experiments on animals but unlikely to be present for humans. But what appears causal in a laboratory rat may be of little relevance to humans.

The short answer to the question, 'when does association mean causation?' is that it is hard to say. It is a judgement. The above criteria can help in the process of judgement, but apart from temporality (to be causal an exposure must precede the disease), none of them present hard and fast rules. This may seem an unsatisfactory situation but it is not an excuse for inaction. This was summed up nicely by Austin Bradford Hill, the British statistician who first suggested the criteria listed above. He wrote:

> All scientific work is incomplete [and] is liable to be upset or modified by advancing knowledge. That does not confer upon us a freedom to ignore the knowledge we already have, or to postpone the action that it appears to demand at a given time.

Summary

Write your own summary using the following questions and headings.

1 What is meant by the terms bias and confounding, and why are they possible explanations for an association found in an epidemiological study?

2 Describe ways in which bias and confounding can be addressed.

3 What is meant by the term 'null hypothesis' and how is it used to assess the roll of chance in explaining an association found in an epidemiological study?

4 How would you assess the causality of an association?

CHAPTER 6

THE DETERMINANTS OF HEALTH AND DISEASE

> What sorts of diseases are the major killers in different parts of the world today?
>
> What does it mean to call something a 'cause' of a disease?
>
> What are the determinants of levels of health in different parts of the world today?

After working through this chapter you should be able to:

- describe the major categories of killing diseases at different times and in different places;

- discuss what is meant by 'demographic and health transitions';

- discuss the concept of 'causes' of diseases;

- give examples of determinants of levels of health in different societies;

- outline a framework for describing the range of determinants of health and disease.

Changing patterns of health and the demographic transition: England as an example

The first ten-yearly national census was taken in 1801, then in 1837 the registration of births and deaths began, making it possible to calculate death rates. From 1874 a doctor's death certificate was required and from then on information about causes of death became available. One reason for starting to collect these data was a growing concern about health as industrialization and urbanization were proceeding rapidly. Peasant farmers and craftsmen and women from the hinterlands and from Ireland were being forced off the land by enclosures and crop failures and were flocking to towns seeking a living. When demand for labour was high, whole families, men, women and children, found work in factories, mines and mills. Consider the health effects of this rural to urban migration in Exercise 6.1.

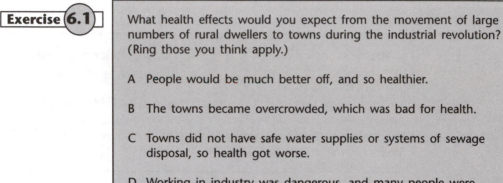

Exercise 6.1

What health effects would you expect from the movement of large numbers of rural dwellers to towns during the industrial revolution? (Ring those you think apply.)

A People would be much better off, and so healthier.

B The towns became overcrowded, which was bad for health.

C Towns did not have safe water supplies or systems of sewage disposal, so health got worse.

D Working in industry was dangerous, and many people were killed, injured or made ill.

E People would be nearer to hospitals and other services, so health would be better.

Health is multifactoral, so no one answer in Exercise 6.1 is complete.

A Some people were certainly better off. Many of the rich and middle classes became richer. The majority, however, the working people, found their living standards swinging up and down, and since they were totally dependent on wages, they were destitute when times were bad and there was no work.
B Social and medical reformers were horrified at urban living conditions. Often whole families shared one room with others, with no facilities. The resulting 'pestilential heap of human beings' provided a breeding ground for many diseases and other problems.
C Slum dwellers often had to depend on fetching water from polluted rivers, and if they had any sanitary facilities at all they were communal overflowing pit middens which drained into those same rivers.
D Many men, women and children died at work or as a result of work. They laboured for long hours beside poorly lit and unguarded machinery, exposed to dust, oils and other hazards.
E There were many charitable dispensaries and hospitals set up, and some Poor Law medical services, but as we shall see later, there was little they could do to prevent or cure these ills of industrialization and urbanization.

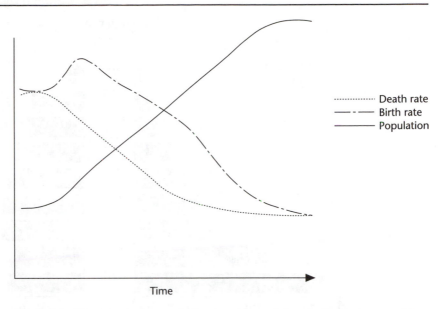

Figure 6.1 Trends in death rates, birth rates and population size in the demographic transition.

Despite the poor health of many town dwellers in nineteenth-century England, overall death rates fell during the decades of industrialization and, with concomitant high birth rates, rapid population growth occurred. There has been much debate on the reasons for this falling death rate (a feature of all countries industrializing in the nineteenth and early twentieth centuries). What is clear, as discussed in Chapter 10, is that health care played little part. McKeown (see Further Reading) argued that increased food supplies were the major factor, as agricultural productivity increased, and improved transport allowed cheaper food, home produced and from the colonies, to reach the markets. People who were better nourished became more resistant to disease.

The fall in death rates was owing largely to a fall in deaths from infectious diseases, especially in infancy and early childhood. Major killers, such as measles, diphtheria, scarlet fever, smallpox and tuberculosis, declined markedly over this period. Cholera made four dramatic appearances in the middle of the nineteenth century before disappearing for good. These four epidemics caused widespread alarm and eventually provided the needed impetus for sanitary reform (for this reason cholera has sometimes been called 'the midwife of public health' in England).

Around 50 years after death rates started to fall dramatically, birth rates also began to show a steady decline. (Initially crude birth rates tend to increase slightly because more women survive to child bearing age: see Figure 6.1.) The combination of falling death rates followed later by falling birth rates resulted in rapid population growth, which then levelled off, and resulted in a dramatic change in the population age structure, to one with a much higher proportion of elderly people. This whole process has been termed the 'demographic transition'. It is illustrated in Figure

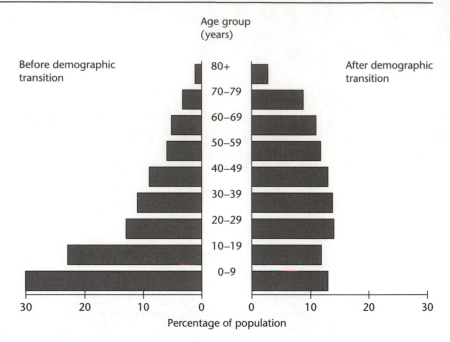

Figure 6.2 Typical population age structures before and after the demographic transition.

6.1 and the population age structures before and after the transition are illustrated in Figure 6.2. This process is common to all countries which have undergone industrialization. In countries which industrialized in the nineteenth century, such as the UK and other Western European countries, this process generally took place over a long period, such as 100 to 150 years. In countries which industrialized in the middle to late twentieth century or are industrializing now this process has tended to occur, or is occurring much more rapidly. Part and parcel of the demographic transition is what has been termed the 'health transition'. This refers to the fact that as rates of infectious disease fall and the population ages, the predominant health problems become those of non-communicable disease, such as cancers, circulatory diseases and diabetes. Clearly, this has major implications for the provision of health services, both public health and individual, as well as much wider implications for the economic and social fabric of a country in trying to meet the health needs of an ageing population.

What patterns of death and disease are found in different parts of the world at the end of the twentieth century?

We will consider two distinct groups of countries. The one we are familiar with in Europe and similar parts of the world is sometimes called 'highly developed' or 'the North', but we will use the World Bank term of established market economies (EME). For the other group, which has been called 'underdeveloped', 'rapidly developing', 'Third World' or 'the South', we will also use a World Bank term, low income Economy (LIE) countries. We will discuss this group of countries first.

Low income economy (LIE) countries

Generally, national data on diseases and causes of death are not available in most LIE countries, but estimates based on partial information, often derived from special studies, are widely used.

Most low income countries have yet to enter or are just entering the demographic transition. Thus rates of communicable diseases remain high. Some communicable diseases, such as malaria and some worm infestations, thrive in a warm climate and are commoner in some of these countries than they have ever been in Europe. They can cause heavy rates of ill health and death. Cholera remains entrenched in parts of Asia, and is now well established wherever sanitary facilities are inadequate in parts of Africa and elsewhere. However, it is other communicable diseases with which we are very familiar which cause the heaviest burdens, such as respiratory and gastrointestinal infections, tuberculosis, measles and other childhood fevers.

Deaths associated with pregnancy, including abortions and childbirth (maternal mortality), are tragically common, with rates up to 30 or more times higher than in EME countries. Trauma and sexually transmitted diseases, most recently HIV infections, cause much disability and death.

Generally, in recent decades there have been falls in infant and child mortality rates, although deterioration seemed to be taking place in some countries in the mid-1980s. Smallpox has been eradicated globally, and where effective immunization programmes have been maintained deaths from measles, tetanus, diphtheria, whooping cough and polio have fallen. Dissemination of knowledge about oral rehydration has led to some reduction in deaths from diarrhoeal diseases in some places, but deaths in childhood and young adulthood from many causes remain very common.

Established market economy (EME) countries

Here the large majority of those born live to a pensionable age and most eventually die of vascular diseases or cancers, the so-called degenerative diseases. Communicable diseases are not now a major cause of premature death in these countries, although many people of all ages suffer from time to time from respiratory and gastrointestinal infections. Against the trends, AIDS deaths are going up everywhere and in some places so are TB deaths, including some in people with HIV infection.

Taking England and Wales as a specific example, we find that among children trauma is now the main killer, followed by congenital abnormalities. In young adults, too, trauma is at the top of the list, followed by suicide. Death rates for men aged between 15 and 44, while low, have been rising recently, with deaths from HIV-associated diseases, suicides and drug and alcohol misuse contributing to this.

From the age group 35 upwards for men and from 55 for women, ischaemic heart disease is the main killer. Up to the age of 75 this is followed by cancers, particularly lung cancer and gut cancers for men, and breast cancer and gut cancers for women, and over 75 stroke becomes second to heart attacks. Lung cancer death rates are beginning to fall for men, but still rising quickly for women.

What causes disease?

We have discussed the diseases which commonly cause deaths in different societies. Now we will look more closely at what causes diseases. This is also discussed, but more briefly, in Chapter 5. Work through Exercise 6.2 now.

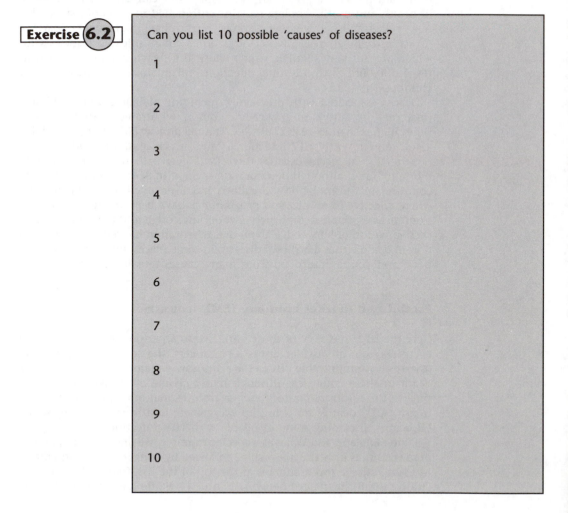

Exercise 6.2

Can you list 10 possible 'causes' of diseases?

1

2

3

4

5

6

7

8

9

10

This question of what causes disease can be answered at several levels. At first glance it may seem easy for some conditions, such as:

Q   What causes the common cold?
A   A virus.

However, if a group of people work in a room where someone has a bad cold, only some of them will catch the cold. Why do you think this is so? See if you can think of three possible reasons before reading on.

1

2

3

You may have mentioned some having immunity because of previous exposure to the virus, some working closer to the cold sufferer and so being more exposed and receiving a bigger dose of virus, some people being run down, some always catching colds etc. In other words, factors may be in the constitution or state of health and resistance of the individual and the size of the exposure.

Let us now consider another room in the same block, where someone also has a cold. In this room, far more of the other workers catch a cold than in the first room. Again try to think of some possible reasons.

1

2

3

You may have thought of things to do with the virus. It may be more virulent than the cold virus in the first room. Or it could be the individuals. They might all be newcomers to the area, few of them having immunity to that virus or all recently returned from long-term sickness, in poor states of nutrition; or all facing redundancy and under severe stress. Alternatively, the environment may differ, the air quality and humidity may favour transmission or the room may be more overcrowded. Or there may be more exposure, because the workers spend more time together than just at work – they travel or live together, or go out together in the evening.

We could repeat the exercise, asking why some people only caught slight colds, while others got bad colds. If we had been discussing a potentially fatal infection instead of a cold, we could ask why some lived and some died. At this point, treatment or management of the condition might come into the discussion.

So causes of the onset of a disease, and its severity in a particular person, at a particular time, can be many.

In classical epidemiology we talk of:

Agent ——————┬—————— Host
                    │
             Environment

For example, using the example of the common cold: the *agent* is the cold virus; factors to do with the *host* include their level of immunity and factors influencing this; and factors to do with the *environment* might include the temperature of the room and how crowded the room is. Look back at the answers you gave above about possible causes of diseases in Exercise 6.2, and try and put a letter by each to clarify which sort of factor it was: agent (A), host (H) or environment (E). The environment is a complex concept, covering much more than physical factors, as we shall see later. Note that an 'agent' need not be an infectious agent. It is just as possible to talk of a carcinogen as being an agent for cancer. You might also note that many non-communicable diseases seem to have many agents, e.g. what is/are the agent(s) causing ischaemic heart disease?

What is meant by a determinant of health or disease in an individual?

One definition is: 'any factor, whether event, characteristic or other definable entity, as long as it brings about a change for the better or the worse in a health condition'. By this definition, any health condition is likely to have many determinants, and any determinant may bring about changes in more than one health condition. The onset of a disease can be seen as part of a web of circumstances, rather than the simple result of one 'cause'.

As is discussed in Chapter 5, a causal factor may be necessary or sufficient, or neither. *Necessary* means that the cause *must* be present for a disease to occur. *Sufficient* cause can refer to a single factor whose presence alone will result in the disease. This is not very common. It can also refer collectively to a group of factors that together will result in the disease. This is much more common, and each factor making up the sufficient cause can be called a *component* cause.

We will now look at health and disease at the *population* level.

What is meant by a determinant of health or disease at a population level?

The same concept of determinants as discussed above is applicable at the community level. However, the nature of the determinants we identify may often be quite different. An attempt to understand what determines the patterns of disease within a population often requires different types of explanation from those for an attempt to understand why a particular individual develops a disease, although clearly the two must be related.

William Farr, the first compiler of statistics at the Registrar-General's Office in London, showed in 1843 that death rates increased with the density of population. The evidence that the chances of life and death are not spread evenly within Britain has been confirmed in all census material produced since then. Although the population structure has changed, the certified causes of death have changed, the death rates have fallen dramatically, our understanding of disease has changed, innumerable new treatments have developed and the National Health Service has been established, inequalities are still found. Such inequalities have been found, too, to a greater or lesser extent, within every country that has been studied, and they can be seen in the stark international health differences between LIE and EME countries.

What are the determinants of poor health in LIE countries?

The most striking difference between the countries with poor health statistics and those with better ones is shown by the World Bank categorizations which we have already used; that is, average poverty and wealth. In the 'low income economies', the average gross national product (GNP) per head per year was 350 dollars in 1991. By contrast, in countries described as having 'established market economies', the range of GNP per head per year in 1991 was from 11,120 dollars in Ireland to 33,610 dollars in Switzerland. Before you read on, see if you can give answers to the questions in Exercise 6.3.

Try to give answers to the following questions.

The main known causes of death in LIE countries, in terms of medical classification of disease, are, as we have seen, communicable diseases. What determinants underlie this fact?

Many of the excess deaths are in children who are suffering from diseases not usually fatal in other parts of the world. Why?

> Some of the killing and disabling diseases are both preventable and treatable, but health services are not effectively preventing or treating them. Why not?

There are many determinants operating upon specific populations, and for particular groups of diseases, but you should have mentioned some of the following points as leading deprived communities to poor health chances. Overall, we are looking at vulnerable communities, heavily exposed to damaging agents, in very unfavourable environments. In deprived areas, levels of malnutrition are high and chronic debilitating diseases are often endemic. The settlements and houses are overcrowded, insanitary and dangerous, exposing the population to trauma and frequent infections and cross-infections. Children have the least resistance and most need protection, so they are the most vulnerable.

In many localities there are no preventive or treatment services within reach, or such services as exist are overstretched by the daily pressures of the sick and are undersupplied and understaffed. They often run out of basic essential drugs. They have no spare capacity to carry out preventive work, and may not be trained how to do it anyway. Such services may charge. Traditional healers may also be scarce, expensive and little inclined to a preventive approach.

Such an analysis, generalized and oversimplified, probably encouraged some experts, including the World Bank, to 'go for growth', to see the solution to health and many other problems as increasing the GNP, in the expectation that resources would 'trickle down' to the poor. Other factors intervened. These included other agendas of some of the outside agencies: banks, donors and big companies whose prime concerns were return on money lent or invested. In addition, there have been disastrous falls in world primary commodity markets, so that rather than having grown, some countries find themselves with unpayable international debts. But even where growth has occurred and the GNP gone up, the 'trickle down' effect has often been disappointing. Such countries may have more rich people, and some have become very rich, but usually the lot and the health of the mass of the poor population has not shown as much improvement as was promised. Where there has been some investment in health, education and transport, it has been disproportionately in the large towns. Teaching hospitals, universities and company and government cars may have flourished, accessible only to the few, but primary health care, universal primary education and a national public transport infrastructure for the many have lagged behind.

The World Bank, which has been party to 'advice' in the past to curtail public expenditure on basic public services, now seems to be modifying its position. The World Development Report for 1993 focuses on the interrelationship between health and development. It identifies the need for policies which ensure income gains for poor households, expanded investment in schooling, particularly for girls, and more emphasis on public health and essential primary health care. It remains to be seen whether such policies can be adopted even by well intentioned countries that are facing economic restructuring and crippling debt burdens and are subject to powerful outside pressures. *In this sense, the determinants of health and disease in these countries are revealed as lying more in the political and economic spheres than in the realms of health knowledge and health care.*

What are the main health determinants in EME countries?

We have already seen that historically in Europe the health of poor town dwellers was worse than the health of others, and that today there are international health differences between poor and rich countries. It is almost self-evident that health and disease, life and death are socially determined when living conditions are appalling and services are poor or non-existent. But one might hope that, in a country like Britain today, things would be different. The majority of people in Britain and other EMEs are well off, compared with nineteenth-century mill workers or twentieth-century shanty town residents, and have access to education, health and welfare services. Surely they should all enjoy equal health chances, except perhaps for a few such as those who must sleep on the streets.

Health statistics reveal that this is not the case. Health inequalities persist in all the 'rich' countries which have been studied. In some the inequalities are increasing, even though 'average' health is improving. Although many of the prevalent causes of death, such as cancers and heart disease, have been called 'diseases of affluence', almost every one of them is commoner in the poor than in the rich members of the affluent society. What is happening is that higher proportions of people in these societies are living to the ages at which cancer and heart disease occur, but these and other diseases are occurring at earlier ages on average in poorer than in richer people. Higher premature death rates in the disadvantaged are found, whatever indicators of relative advantage and disadvantage are used. They are found in death rates for babies, children, younger adults and older people, for both men and women. There is no threshold. The most advantaged are healthiest, the least advantaged are sickest, and those in between have in between health. These gradients are so well known that they are sometimes taken as given, and investigators looking for causal factors for diseases 'match' or 'control' for social class etc.

This may sometimes be appropriate, but it overlooks some burning questions. Why do these social class and related differences occur? Try to give some possible explanations in Exercise 6.4.

Suggest some possible reasons for differences in health between
different social classes in established market economy countries.

There are no easy answers in Exercise 6.4. 'Lifestyle' explanations are
often given, such as that people in lower socio-economic groups have
poorer diets, and smoke and drink more. Undoubtedly, in many countries such factors do play a part. But there are also many studies showing
that such factors can only explain part of the difference between socio-
economic groups. There is currently much research into what other factors
account for the differences.

Sally Macintyre (see Further Reading) has given us a framework with
which to study the processes and interrelationships at different levels of
the continuum which determines health and disease, from: 'at the one
end, macropolitical and economic characteristics of a society; through
cultural, economic and social features . . . of communities; through social
circumstances and dynamics . . . through individual psychological traits
and processes . . . through physical functioning of body systems . . . and
ultimately through to the cellular and molecular level, at the other end.'

Here we will focus mainly on the macropolitical and economic levels,
and look at the evidence assembled by Wilkinson (see Further Reading).
His analysis of statistics on wealth and health inequalities in EME countries points the way towards strategies to reduce health inequalities.
Wilkinson found that standards of health are strongly associated with
how equal or unequal incomes are in a society. Countries with the longest
life expectancies are those with the smallest spread of incomes, and this is
not just owing to the minority living in poverty pulling down the average in the more unequal countries. The middle and upper income groups
also compare unfavourably with their equivalents in less unequal countries. Further, in those countries where wealth inequalities have increased
over recent decades, health indices have slipped behind those of otherwise
comparable countries where wealth inequalities have decreased. Wilkinson
has demonstrated that the health of all of us appears to be damaged
when the poor get relatively or absolutely poorer. He notes that in these
same societies with increasing inequalities, other aspects of quality of life
are also deteriorating for most people. The growth of unemployment,
robbery, violence and addictions, the decay of our cities and the growing alienation among the young have an impact on everyone. Factors
like loss of social cohesion and the growth of feelings of insecurity may
be influencing everyone's health and well being.

We can conclude that any strategy which seeks to improve the health
of a nation is unlikely to succeed if it is restricted to health promotion
and health service issues alone. Addressing wealth inequalities needs to be
part of addressing health inequalities.

Macintyre's framework describes many other levels at which determinants of health and disease operate, in addition to the macropolitical and economic issues just discussed. Public health practice needs to be concerned with the others too. Particular attention is given to the community and individual levels in Chapter 7.

Summary

Use the following questions to write a summary to this chapter.

1 What happens to death rates, birth rates, causes of death and population age structure when a population passes through the demographic transition?

2 Discuss the concept of 'causes' of disease in relation to individuals and to communities or populations.

3 Use the following headings to list determinants of your health.

(a) Determinants to do with you as an individual.

(b) Determinants to do with your immediate physical and social environment.

 (c) Determinants to do with your wider social, political and physical environment (go up to national and even international levels if you feel that it is appropriate).

CHAPTER 7

HEALTH PROMOTION

What do we mean by the term health promotion?

Is health promotion the same as health education?

Are there different types of or approaches to health promotion?

Who should take responsibility for promoting health – state or individual?

After working through this chapter you should be able to:

- identify the different types of activity and care approaches which come under the heading of health promotion;

- distinguish the activities of health education, health protection and health promotion;

- describe five models of health education;

- identify individual and collective responsibilities for health and debate where the balance should lie.

What do we mean by the term health promotion?

Health promotion is a term that has grown in popularity recently. It is certainly a frequently used word in the politician's vocabulary and the media bombard us with health promoting advice and information. The term is being applied to cover a number of different issues and activities, which may be broadly similar, but which actually also have some very significant differences. We need to consider exactly what we mean by the term and what types of activities come under its heading.

In order to understand the term it is important to appreciate that there are two words in the phrase 'health' and 'promotion'. It would be inappropriate to spend time trying to define health; suffice it to say that the definition used sets the parameters for what is to be promoted. Work through Exercise 7.1 now.

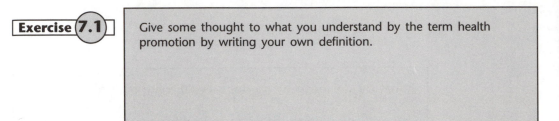

Exercise 7.1

Give some thought to what you understand by the term health promotion by writing your own definition.

Your definition may have included:

- aspects of physical, psychological and social health;
- prevention of disease processes;
- development of fitness;
- individual, group or society activities;
- education relating to health matters;
- achievement of individual or community health potential.

It would not be surprising if your definition gave considerable focus to healthy lifestyle issues, because this is a very common interpretation of health promotion. However, it is a mistake to think that spreading the word about healthy lifestyle options is all that health promotion is about.

Compare your definition with one produced by the World Health Organization (WHO) in 1986.

Health promotion is the process of enabling people to increase control over, and to improve, their health . . . Health is a positive concept emphasising social and personal resources, as well as physical capacities. Therefore, health promotion is not just the responsibility of the health sector, but goes beyond healthy lifestyles to well-being.

The WHO has incorporated this approach in a major initiative called Health for All by the Year 2000, known as HFA. This sets objectives to reduce inequalities in health between and within nations. The WHO definition widens the definition of health promotion considerably from the healthy lifestyle focus.

Some key factors you might want to think about are:

- How are people 'enabled', and what does this mean?
- If it is not just the responsibility of the health sector, who else has responsibility?

What types of activities fall under the umbrella of health promotion?

Let us explore some of the components of health promotion further. We are all exposed to 'health promotion' in several different forms:

- on an individual basis;
- as part of a targeted group, e.g. by gender, age or lifestyle;
- initiated by the individual;
- imposed on the individual;
- in changes to the wider environment in which we live.

To consider the components of health promotion further, work through Exercise 7.2.

Exercise 7.2

> Think about your own experiences and list how and when you consider you were exposed to health promotion. Go as far back or as recently as you wish.

Your list probably includes aspects of health maintenance, health education, health enhancement and illness prevention. Health promotion is commonly used interchangeably with these other terms. Health promotion may include elements of all these activities, not as an aim in themselves, but as a means of promoting optimum wellness. Let us give some consideration to what we mean by some of the terms we have identified.

Health education can be thought of as giving information or instruction, or enhancing understanding about health. This could take the form of education about our health potential and about how to attain it or about how to avoid certain ill health problems.

Examples of this approach include:

- advising parents about child care and development so that they can take appropriate child safety measures and so reduce the risk of accidents;
- encouraging adults to restrict their alcohol intake to avoid ill health consequences and/or road traffic accidents;

Think of another example that is relevant to your interests.

You may have noticed that a significant amount of health education effort focus on negative or ill health. In other words, it does not focus on enhancing health, but preventing or correcting health problems, e.g. encouraging participation in exercise to prevent coronary heart disease or as part of a rehabilitation programme after coronary heart problems have been experienced. This is closely related to the next category: ill health prevention.

Ill health prevention can be thought of as increasing understanding of the factors contributing to the development of ill health, so that preventive action may be taken to avoid or reduce exposure to them. Several types of activities could be involved:

- screening to identify disease at an early stage;
- developmental surveillance of the child population to identify deviations from normal at an early stage;
- increasing understanding of the causality of certain diseases and possible preventative actions, e.g. dental caries and diet, cigarette smoking and lung disease;
- immunization against certain diseases;
- hormone replacement therapy to relieve menopausal symptoms and/or prevent osteoporosis and cardiovascular disease.

Again, identify some examples of your own.

Illness prevention activities are often categorized into at least three distinct levels. You will see these used frequently, although different authors often use different definitions. The definitions used here are based on epidemiological terms.

- Primary prevention: action to prevent disease occurring, i.e. to reduce its incidence.
- Secondary prevention: action to reduce the prevalence of a disease by shorting its duration, i.e. curing people who have the disease. Much screening activity, such as screening for breast cancer, is secondary prevention in that it aims to pick up the disease in its early stages so as to gain a better chance of effecting a cure.
- Tertiary prevention: action aimed at reducing the complications (including disability and handicap) of a disease. Rehabilitation of individuals after a stroke is an example of tertiary prevention.

Health maintenance actions can be thought of as those activities that protect our health status. Examples include:

- to continue the child theme, legislation regarding the materials used in toy production;
- road safety crossings;
- supporting and encouraging a mother to continue to breastfeed her baby;
- reinforcing good dietary habits.

Models of health education and health promotion

Let us take the issues a stage further by exploring the activities of health education and ill health prevention in more detail. In your list of health promotion you consider you have been exposed to (Exercise 7.2) you may have included a variety of approaches, some telling you what to do, some increasing your knowledge about health options. There are several models of health education. Although some have overlapping aims, we will attempt to distinguish them according to: (a) the overall goal guiding the model; (b) whether it is the professional or the client who sets the agenda.

Medical model/negative health model

Health education based on this model usually has a disease or disability as its focus. It is concerned with:

- informing people, e.g. about the dangers of smoking in relation to lung disease;
- high-risk individuals taking up screening services, e.g. HIV, cholesterol, breast.

Add an example relevant to your particular specialism.

In this type of health education the health care professional often takes on the role of expert adviser or information giver. Communication is often in one direction only, i.e. professional to client or patient. The impetus for developing this type of health education programme may be a high incidence of a particular disease. A useful exercise would be to identify national and/or local health education campaigns and to try to identify why they were developed at a particular time.

Behaviour change or modification model

This approach focuses on encouraging individuals to change their behaviour to increase their chances of avoiding ill health or of developing a better level of health. It usually focuses on the adoption of a healthy lifestyle. We are often bombarded with this approach, e.g. stop smoking, drink in moderation, practise safe sex, eat low fat/high fibre diets. People may sometimes feel they are being 'told' what to do and that they are at fault if they do not follow the advice: does this sound familiar in relation to smoking? This approach appears to have two underlying assumptions; that health status is determined by individual behaviour and that individuals can choose to change their behaviour *and* have the resources to do so, if they are advised of the healthy alternatives. We will explore this idea in more detail later, but think back to the WHO definition we looked at earlier. That seemed to lay considerable store in health promotion, including enabling people to take a healthy option, and this requires more than information or advice giving.

Informed choice model

This approach is more concerned with increasing knowledge and understanding so that individuals can make the most appropriate choice for their situation, often referred to as an informed choice. Although there appears to be more partnership with the client in this approach, it is usually the professional or state who chooses which subject will be addressed. For example, it may be the National Curriculum or the school governors that decide if sexual health education will be part of school education. There is an assumption here that everyone has equal opportunities to make an informed choice. We will return to this issue later.

Client-focused model

The ownership of the interaction is much more with the client in this model. This approach should be responsive to what the client wants to know or consider. The client, not the health professional, sets the agenda. This approach has much in common with community development approaches to care. It sounds good and appears to avoid some of the pitfalls we have identified in the other models. It means that the client's priorities, interests and concerns are addressed, but we have not found perfection, as there are still some potential problems. An important point to consider is whether we always know what we need to know. Is it fair to leave agenda setting solely to the client? What about issues they are unaware of or chose to avoid? What should be done about them?

Collective or societal model

This model moves away from the individual level and takes on a societal approach to health education, prevention and promotion. It may involve political or legislative issues, e.g. seat belt use or the provision of cycle paths. As a consequence of the use of this model it may be easier for individuals to choose the healthy option or to fulfil their health potential (e.g. provision of leisure facilities, subsidized rates for leisure facilities) or it may enhance the population's chances of not encountering a negative health risk and increasing their chances of being able to pursue a healthy lifestyle. This model generally operates on a longer time scale than the other models we have discussed.

The type of actions people working with this model might take include the following.

- Protecting in a preventive way, e.g. provision of clean water supply, supplementing certain food with extra minerals and vitamins.
- Protecting in an educative way: this could be directed towards policy makers by lobbying politicians or service providers for a particular service or legislation; it could also relate to general dissemination to the public about a health care issue, e.g. the mass education and publicity campaign associated with the discovery of HIV or action to prevent 'cot deaths'.
- Protecting against negative health effects, e.g. legislation regarding levels of lead emissions from car exhausts.

Identify another couple of examples of the collective approach to health promotion.

It may not be immediately obvious how health care workers can be involved in this type of activity. You need to think about care moving away from the one-to-one level and consider the health care worker as someone whose role is to identify and stimulate awareness of health needs, whether that be at an individual, community, national or international level.

To consider how these different models might apply to some specific health issues work through Exercise 7.3.

Using the grid below, consider which of these models might be useful (several may be used over varying time scales) to address the health issues from varying perspectives. There are a couple of blank spaces to use with your own examples.

	Medical	Behaviour change	Informal choice	Client-focused	Collective or societal
Smoking					
Diet					
HIV					
Accident prevention					
Stress management					
Ability to deal with personal development (adolescence/ ageing)					
Controlling car exhaust emissions					
_____					
_____					

Why is advice on health often ignored?

We have identified a wide range of health promoting activities that we may meet as part of our everyday life. It seems appropriate to question why we still have large numbers of people who do not achieve their health potential. Why do people not follow this widely available advice, and take up the services on offer which could possibly enhance their health status? This brings us back to something we touched on earlier. Is everyone able to take the healthy option? Is health promotion addressed at the right level? Should it lie exclusively in the individual's hands? How much responsibility should the state take for the health of individuals? Where should the balance lie?

Let us focus on you. Work through Exercise 7.4.

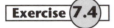

Exercise 7.4

It is fairly safe to assume that you have considerable knowledge about what is healthy lifestyle practice in relation to diet, alcohol consumption, exercise etc., but have you modified your behaviour in line with your knowledge base? Make a list of health advice you know but do not follow (only a brief summary) and try to identify the reasons.

What about other people, such as clients, patients or family and friends? Also try to identify reasons why they do or do not follow the vast volumes of advice on health.

One reason you might have identified in Exercise 7.4 is that everyone is not immediately receptive to, for example, health education. Giving a 'healthy message' is not always the most appropriate starting point. Often people need to be motivated and empowered to consider their health before they can begin to think about making some commitment to promote their health. People need to consider that their health is important, that they can improve it, that they have options. Clients may need to be helped to raise their self-esteem or feelings of self-worth in order to have the confidence to set their own agenda and be active participants in the health promoting process. We are really talking about empowerment of individuals or communities, a key feature of the enabling process referred to earlier. Another prerequisite of people acting on health promotion advice is that they can develop the necessary skills to do so. Modern school programmes are based on skill enhancement, such as how to handle peer group pressure, developed through workshops, role playing and other participatory methods.

How broad is the scope of health promotion?

We have focused largely on the individual level, but health promotion is much wider than individual issues and individual actions. It is concerned with global warming, food preservation, crop production, engineering investment to achieve less pollution, transport policies and allocation of resources to different sectors of health care services. The message is that health promotion combines a wide number of issues, which complement each other to assist with the achievement of better levels of health. Some will have as their focus the prevention of ill health, some the protection and maintenance of current health levels, others an attempt to achieve higher levels of health for individuals and to reduce the variation in health status across populations.

The impact of any action or policy aimed at promoting health can often be limited if it is only focused on one perspective. Health is a multi-factorial concept, and actions that include several routes to achieving the aim of promoting health are often more successful. Use Exercise 7.5 to help you to think through some of the many ways in which public policy can influence health.

Identify some national policy changes over the last ten years and consider their impact on health. You may wish to consider such things as transport and road policy, changes to the organization of health care, changes in education, policies towards the unemployed and so on.

Conclusion: what is health promotion?

Let us return to our original question: what is health promotion? We might now want to think of it as:

- an umbrella term whose facets include ill health prevention activities, health education and health protection, but whose aim is achieving the highest potential levels of health and not merely avoiding ill health;
- an activity that incorporates prevention, education and protection.

Client participation in health promotion activities may be of varying types:

Passive _____ Active

Participation may be within individuals' choice or they may need to be assisted or empowered to participate.

Finally, health promoting actions may be taken at an individual or collective level. A collective level could be on a worldwide perspective.

Summary

Write your own summary of this chapter by addressing the following questions.

1 Write a short paragraph to distinguish between the activities of health education, health protection and health promotion.

2 Briefly describe the key features of the five models of health education.

3 Write a short paragraph which summarizes how you see yourself, as a health care professional, being involved in health promotion (either now or in the future).

CHAPTER 8

HEALTH NEEDS ASSESSMENT

What is a health need?

Can we assess health needs at a wider level than the individual or family?

How can we identify what are the health needs of a particular community?

How do health needs differ between groups and localities?

After working through this chapter you should be able to:

- define different types of need;

- identify different units for the analysis of health needs;

- list the functions of a community health need assessment;

- describe a framework for the process of community health profiling;

- list possible sources of data which can be used to inform the pro-filing process.

What is involved in health needs assessment?

Several concepts and activities are involved in assessing or profiling health needs. There are at least five issues for consideration:

- what definition or interpretation of health are we using;
- what a health need is;
- what kind of information we need to make the assessment;
- where we access the data to provide the information;
- what we do with the information to make an assessment.

The issues involved here, health and need, are not absolute concepts and are relative to the time and people concerned. Between individuals, groups and regions there will be differing definitions and prioritization of health and what a health need is. As our expectations of health and health care availability change, so do our definitions.

What is health?

There are many definitions of health, but it will suffice for this discussion to say that health has physical, social and psychological components and it is not a static but a dynamic concept. Although we will look at the idea of need and health need in more detail later, let us use the health need idea to explore further the question of what is health. We will do this by working through Exercise 8.1.

Exercise 8.1

Consider the following statements:

A   A health need exists when health is absent.

B   No matter how healthy they are, everyone has health needs.

C   Health needs can be predicted by factors such as age, gender and social position.

D   If you are unaware of your health need, that means it must not be important.

Which do you agree with?   A   B   C   D

Compare your responses in Exercise 8.1 with the following comments.

A This represents a fairly narrow view of health, i.e. health is the absence of disease. What about health in terms of well being or achieving individual health potential?
B This is probably the nearest to the truth. All individuals have health needs, either to maintain health or to improve their level of health.

C This is a rather impractical statement at the individual level, though relevant at the population level. It is true to say, for example, that many women might benefit from certain intervention programmes, such as cervical screening, but from a particular woman's point of view her health needs are dynamic and individual. This emphasizes the skill of the practitioner who is assisting with the discovery of need.

D This statement doesn't really hold water. Unless you have knowledge of your health needs you cannot make an informed choice of whether to act on them or not.

Let us explore the issue of need in more detail.

What is a need?

If we think about how we become aware that we have a need, that will help us to develop our definition of the word. Start by working through Exercise 8.2.

> Think about any needs you have had recently, possibly but not necessarily related to health. List them. Next to each one describe how you came to identify it as a need, e.g. was it based on specialist advice, on something you read, on peer group pressure, on feeling unwell and so on.

Your responses in Exercise 8.2 probably indicated several different ways of identifying needs. We can identify some of these by considering, as an example, some possible responses to the question: 'what needs might I have in relation to my car?'

1 The car has recently had an MOT test and the mechanic told me that the exhaust must be replaced.
2 The car exhaust is becoming noisy and I think it will have to be replaced shortly.
3 My friend has the same age car as mine and has had to have the exhaust replaced, so mine will probably need replacing soon as well.

Now let us try to categorize these responses:

1 Someone makes you aware of a need you had not actually identified yourself.
2 You may be aware of a need yourself and may or may not do something about it. Have you ever had toothache, but not gone to the dentist?

3 You may only become aware of a need if you compare your situation with someone else.

We can now try to relate this discussion to health and look at four levels of health need that have been identified by Bradshaw (see Further Reading). Each type of need is listed below with examples, together with a space to allow you to add an example or examples of your own.

Normative need: what the expert or professional defines as a need.
Example: the medical definition of overweight and obesity.
Example:

Felt need: a need that can be equated with a want.
Example: the desire to lose weight.
Example:

Expressed need: a need or want that is translated into action.
Example: seeking advice about weight reduction.
Example:

Comparative need: need identified by comparing the services received by one group of individuals with those received by a similar group.
Example: a group for whom no weight reducing advice is available compared to a similar group that has a service.
Example:

You will have realized that the situation can become extremely complex when there is a lack of awareness or a disagreement between the parties involved in defining a health need. These parties could be professional and client, client and client, client and government policy maker, social worker and nurse, doctor and health visitor. For example, some one may desire to lose weight when from a medical point of view his or her weight is perfectly normal; a group may demand access to a particular weight reducing service because the service is available elsewhere, but there may be no evidence that the treatment does any good. This latter example illustrates that the problem lies not only with the identification of need but also with deciding when a need has been met. We return again to the problem of how we measure health.

Measurements of health

There are many different approaches to measuring health, reflecting the fact that health is a multidimensional concept. The commonest approach is to use mortality and, where they exist, morbidity rates from specific diseases. National targets for improvements in health may define reductions over a given time period in disease-specific mortality rates. For example, one of the targets in the Health of the Nation initiative in England and Wales was 'To reduce death rates for both coronary heart disease and stroke in people under 65 by at least 40 per cent by the year 2000'.

An example of a different approach is that taken by Townsend, Phillimore and Beattie (see Further Reading) in their study of health and deprivation. Rather than using specific diseases, i.e. stroke or suicide, they used the following dimensions of health:

- death registrations;
- birth weight indicators;
- permanent sickness rates.

They combined these to form an 'overall health index' and, because they acknowledged that health is affected by social circumstances, they also developed a deprivation index using census information on unemployment, car ownership, home ownership and overcrowding. Some data following this approach for health districts in the north-east of England are shown in Exercise 8.3. Look at this now.

Exercise 8.3

Look at the data, then consider the question below.

District	Health score	Deprivation score
Hartlepool	3.25	2.02
North Tees	1.60	−1.67
South Tees	0.70	0.96
Northumberland	−3.94	−3.25
Gateshead	2.59	3.73
Newcastle	1.59	3.70
North Tyneside	0.64	0.41
Sunderland	0.27	3.73

The higher scores indicate greater ill health and deprivation. Zero equals the average.

What inferences can you draw from this chart about the relationship between social circumstances and health status?

In your response to Exercise 8.3 you may have included some of the following comments.

- It appears that health and deprivation may be linked. Northumberland appears to have high levels of health and low levels of deprivation. North Tyneside appears to have a slightly higher than average level of deprivation and a similarly lower than average health status.
- The correlation between deprivation and health scores is not consistent. Hartlepool's health score is rather worse than the deprivation score.
- Some areas appear to have a health score better than expected, in view

of the deprivation score. Sunderland's health score is just below average but the deprivation score is considerably above average.

In order to make more sense of these scores we would need to know more about the areas, such as their response to deprivation, and whether deprivation has been long term or a recent event. We would also need to investigate how well these scores actually reflect the health and social circumstances of the people living in those health districts.

So far we have examined definitions of health and need and very briefly touched on the measurement of health. We need to put all these issues together to consider health needs assessment.

Health needs assessment

Health needs assessment can be carried out from multiple levels and perspectives. This is illustrated in Figure 8.1. Let us work through some of the issues surrounding health needs assessment from different perspectives. Before we can embark on any assessment process we need to be aware of the overall goal of the process, which will guide the process in both a qualitative and quantitative manner. Look at Exercise 8.4.

Exercise 8.4

Consider the following goals. Think through the type of assessment processes you might use to help you achieve, and know whether you have achieved, each of these goals.

- To reduce deaths from coronary heart disease by 20 per cent by the year 2000.

- To reduce the number of children with dental caries by 15 per cent by the year 2000.

- To add years to life and life to years.

- To provide a service that is responsive to the demands of the users of the service.

The first two goals in Exercise 8.4 are to do with mortality and morbidity, respectively, from medically defined diseases. Health needs assessment to assist in the achievement of these goals might concentrate on rates of these conditions and identified risk factors for them. The third goal refers not only adding years to life but also to 'adding life to years'. This could be interpreted simply in terms of reducing the prevalence of disease

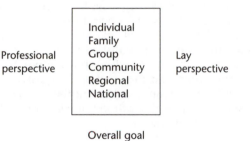

Figure 8.1 Levels and perspectives in health needs assessments.

in older age, or might be interpreted more broadly and positively in terms of adding to the quality of life in other ways as well. Clearly, which interpretation is used will make a big difference as to how 'health needs' are defined and assessed. Finally, assessing health needs with the aim of providing a more client-oriented service will mean that we need to find out what clients want, what they think of the current service and so on. None of these approaches is mutually exclusive. The point is simply that the type of information required depends upon what it is we want to achieve.

There are many examples of health needs assessment carried out at different levels. Many countries have strategies for the improvement of the nation's health. These strategies are based on some sort of assessment of the nation's health needs. An old example is the 1976 publication in the United Kingdom of *Prevention and Health: Everybody's Business*. In this, four needs were identified: those of an ageing population and those owing to environmental and social conditions, adverse lifestyle and mental health needs. These were arrived at from examination of the following data:

- mortality figures;
- hospital admissions data;
- time off work for sickness;
- data from primary health care;
- data showing demographic patterns;
- data on health-related behaviours, such as smoking, alcoholism, use of leisure.

The scope for prevention was identified by:

- comparison with other countries, principally Sweden;
- comparison between areas and regions within the UK;
- comparisons between social classes.

Together with targets at a national level, we need to be able to identify and meet health needs at more local levels. How do we do this? It would be virtually impossible to make an individual health needs assessment on all of the population, and one would have to question if it were really necessary or whether intermediate levels between nation and individual level would be most appropriate. A number of approaches have been taken. The levels at which health needs assessment is carried out often reflect the administrative units for the provision of social and health services. The health needs assessment can then serve the purpose of guiding the provision of the health and social services in that area. An advantage of using such administrative units is that many statistics, such as census information and mortality rates, are published for those areas. A disadvantage is that the units may not equate with what the population considers to be a 'natural' community and may contain very diverse populations living under very different circumstances. Another option is to base a health needs assessment on a neighbourhood or community. We will now explore this type of unit of analysis.

Community health profiling

Again we need to consider some of the components of the idea before we look at the process. How can we identify a community: can we set boundaries from a map; is it determined by the organization of primary health services or by the schools the children attend? Can it actually be described in geographical terms or must it also have a subjective element of belonging? Consider some of these issues for yourself by working through Exercise 8.5.

 Exercise 8.5

> Think about yourself. List the community or communities you belong to. For each one give the reasons why you consider yourself a member of that community.

There are many possibilities you may have considered in Exercise 8.5.

- The housing estate. Two housing estates could be situated very close together, but depending on the different types of housing, the inhabitants may see themselves as belonging to one community spread over two estates or to two different communities.
- The area of the town in which you live. This may be the east or west part of a town, the inner city or the suburbs etc.
- Geographical boundaries. Communities may be determined by the presence of a river, major road network etc.
- Your place of work and/or job. You may consider that you belong to two communities, your place of work and your home, or they may be one and the same, particularly if you live near your work and many of your neighbours work at the same place.
- Your religious group and/or your place of worship.
- Your ethnic group. It may be that you consider yourself part of a wider

community embracing all members of your ethnic group across an area, or just the people of the same ethnic group in your immediate area.

- Your age group, such as 20s, over 40s etc.
- Your civil state, i.e. married with children, married without children, single parent, single without children etc.
- Your sexual orientation.
- Your political beliefs and activities.
- And so on.

Now that we have identified what might be a 'community', we need to consider why we might want to profile it.

Why profile community health?

Although general levels of health have improved over the years, there is still plenty of room for further development. There is a wide variation in the levels of health achieved in different communities, e.g. rural, inner city, by socio-economic status. There is an argument that suggests that taking a reactive approach to health care contributes to this situation, i.e. the emphasis is on dealing with problems and issues when they arise rather than trying to anticipate and respond to them at an earlier stage. Particularly with the growing interest in the public health movement, there have been calls for a change in approach to one that is more proactive in identifying locality health needs and responding specifically to them.

Community nurses, particularly health visitors, have always worked with groups and communities with the intention of identifying the health needs of those communities, involving varying amounts of community collaboration over time. In the early days of health visiting in the UK, the work was concentrated on those areas with obvious health needs, such as areas of poverty. There are still areas of obvious poverty in the UK and other industrialized countries, but in many areas health needs have become less obvious. There has been a need to develop skills in assessing health care needs for two related reasons: first, because without an assessment process many needs may be missed; second, the desire to use limited health resources for a community in the most effective way.

Let us think next of some of the ways in which the local community or area in which you live can affect your health. Consider this in Exercise 8.6.

List the ways in which you feel that the local community or area in which you live has, or could have, an influence on your health. List positive and negative influences.

Depending on your particular community and the perspective you have adopted, you may have highlighted some of the following:

- employment availability, together with easy access to work and/or major services;
- adequacy and accessibility of services such as health, education and social services;
- appropriateness and quality of housing to suit your needs;
- people around for support and social contact;
- levels of crime and vandalism, and how safe you feel;
- accessibility of recreational activities;
- transport facilities and networks;
- the pleasantness and quality of the local environment.

The community in which you live can obviously have a significant influence on your health, and profiling the community may therefore highlight health needs. The needs identified by profiles may serve several functions. For example, a profile can increase understanding and knowledge of an area in order to make an objective and systematic health needs assessment rather than rely on preconceived ideas. People are often guilty of making assumptions, such as that an affluent area will not have a problem with child abuse, whereas we appear to be more ready to acknowledge the possibility of its existence in a more deprived area, or that only mothers at the higher end of the social scale will breastfeed. However, in reality such broad generalizations are not true. As with all health care interventions, a systematic assessment of needs is essential. The clear message here is that an objective search for health needs has to be performed. This should be done in partnership with the population because of the relative definitions of need and health that the professional and lay person may hold.

We have identified how the community can affect health and the purpose of a community health needs assessment. We now need to explore *how* to profile the health needs of a community.

The process of community health profiling

As we have already identified, health needs assessments and community profiling may be carried out for different reasons. It is impossible to give a standard format for the process. However, there are certain key issues that will always need to be addressed, although the emphasis will vary. Many community health workers have developed their own frameworks to guide their profiling activities and it may be worth contacting your community health workers in your area. Some examples are provided in the suggested reading for this chapter. It is important to state clearly that performing a community profile is not just a data collection exercise. Amassing copious amounts of data about an area is not sufficient to make a health needs assessment. As with any other nursing or health care activity, you must understand the data and be able to apply them in order to define needs, set targets for health and actions to achieve them, implement a plan of actions and evaluate the outcome.

	Positive or negative resource	Indicators/factors
Environment		Local industry, maps, accident rates, crime/vandalism.
Housing		Observation, local authority, housing associations, homeless figures, hostels.
Demography		Census data, caseload, practice profiles.
Social class		Occupations, lifestyle, values.
Transport		Car ownership, public transport, cost.
Shops		Range of goods, price levels, accessibility.
Religious groups		Types, location, attendance, resources.
Leisure facilities		Recreation facilities, pubs, restaurants, costs, accessibility, sports teams, cubs, guides, parks.
Education		Pre-school, school, adult, location, cost.
Health care		Hospital and primary care, location, accessibility, patient participation, organization of nursing services, alternative therapies, user representatives, e.g. Community Health Council.
Voluntary		Church groups, support groups, self-help groups.
Character		History, warmth, friendliness, style, design, residents' opinions.
Family structures		Mobile population, single parents, lone elderly, working parents.
Economics		Unemployment level, overcrowding, affluence, poverty.

Figure 8.2 A framework for community profiling.

A profiling framework is presented here (Figure 8.2), identifying key factors in the community which may influence health in a positive or negative way. Being too prescriptive with respect to a profiling tool defeats the purpose of the exercise. This particular framework may not be the most suitable tool to use to profile all communities. However, it is possible to adapt the framework by, for example, supplementing headings that are particularly applicable to an area and then making an estimation of the resources and deficits in a particular community.

It is important to realize that the population being profiled must be involved in the process in order to avoid only identifying overt needs. The worker(s) carrying out the profile must therefore be able to engage the local population in the process. This necessitates being familiar with the community and being able to identify local sources of information to develop the profile in partnership. Identifying the resources of an area is only one part of a community health profile. In addition, the profiler must have the knowledge and skill to make an assessment of the health needs of the area based on the information gathered and on routinely available local and national data, such as:

- census information;
- mortality rates;
- birth rates;
- morbidity data;
- service utilization, e.g. immunization rates, cervical cytology rates;
- national patterns of demography;
- information on society values and changes in family life structure;
- government policy on pollution, housing, benefit levels, community care.

What happens after assessment?

An action plan to meet the identified needs should be the next level of activity. This would be followed by evaluation of the impact of the implementation of the action plan as part of an assessing, planning, implementing and evaluating cycle. If needs cannot be met, for whatever reason, it is important that they are none the less documented and acknowledged as part of a dynamic profiling process.

Summary

Respond to questions below and complete your own summary of this chapter.

1 Health needs assessment is a dynamic process which may be undertaken at an individual, community or national level. Give an example of an assessment carried out at these different levels.

Individual _____

Community _____

National _____

2 There are different types of acknowledged and unacknowledged need and there may be differences between professional and lay opinions. List four types of need and give an example of each that relates specifically to your area of health care.

(a)

(b)

(c)

(d)

3 The community (used here in the sense of the area in which one lives) can have significant influences on health. Give three examples of how a community can affect health positively and three examples of how it could have a negative effect on health.

Positive

(a)

(b)

(c)

Negative

(a)

(b)

(c)

4 Profiling involves the systematic collection and analysis of data. List six sources of data that would inform the profiling process. Include both qualitative and quantitative sources.

(a)

(b)

(c)

(d)

(e)

(f)

5 In order to complete a health needs assessment for a whole community it may be necessary to apply this framework to several groups within the community, so as to come up with an overall health needs assessment and priorities for action. Consider this list of possible residents:

• active elderly lady, caring for her husband who suffers with dementia;
• young mother with two children under 5 years old;
• adolescent from social class IV household;
• 40-year-old single employed woman;
• recently retired couple;
• young adult with a learning disability, living with his or her family.

Using a community you are familiar with, such as an area you are studying, living in or working in:

(a) apply the profiling framework from the point of view of three of the individual case histories presented above;

(b) indicate how and from where you would access the necessary data.

A blank profiling framework is provided which could be photocopied for further use.

Blank community profiling framework

	Positive or negative resource	Indicators/factors
Environment		
Housing		
Demography		
Social class		
Transport		
Shops		
Religious groups		
Leisure facilities		
Education		
Health care		
Voluntary groups		
Character		
Family structures		
Economics		

CHAPTER 9

PRINCIPLES OF SCREENING

What do we mean by 'screening'?

Why screen for one disease and not another?

How are decisions made about who will benefit from the screening?

Do those at risk always take up the screening on offer?

After working through this chapter you should be able to:

- define screening and understand how it differs from surveillance or case identification;

- identify different types of screening and the rationale for their selection;

- understand how the population that will benefit from screening is identified;

- list the criteria or principles for a screening programme;

- list some of the factors that may influence the uptake of available screening.

What is screening?

Screening is in essence about looking for health problems, but if it is not planned and carried out correctly, it can be an ineffective, inappropriate and unethical attempt at health care. We first need to clarify exactly what we mean by the term 'screening'.

Screening is a commonly, although sometimes imprecisely, used term. By comparing and contrasting it with some other health care activities, it is possible to identify its key components. Do this in Exercise 9.1.

Exercise 9.1

Consider the following statements:

A   Screening is a diagnostic activity.

B   Screening is an identification process.

C   Screening is about identifying disease at an early stage.

D   Screening is concerned with health status improvement for the individual.

Which statement(s) most accurately describe(s) screening?

A   B   C   D

A Screening may identify someone who needs to be referred for further investigation. Screening is not a substitute for diagnosis, it is a different and distinct activity.
B This is a good description of screening, a process of identifying those at risk of some health status threat. Diagnosis to establish the existence of disease or precursor to a disease should follow.
C Screening is indeed about identifying disease at an early stage so that treatment can be instigated and the prognosis improved. However, screening is also used to identify individuals at risk from developing a disease some time in the future so that preventive action can take place to prevent the occurrence of the problem.
D It is true to say that screening is carried out for individual benefit but that is only part of the story. For example, screening also has a role in the control of infectious disease, in that it can be used to identify the carrier of a disease in the community, such as tuberculosis. Screening is often established on the basis of whether it will improve the health of the population.

These issues are well summed up in this definition of screening: 'The presumptive identification of unrecognised disease or defect by the application of tests, examinations or other procedures which can be applied rapidly. Screening tests sort out the apparently well persons who probably have a disease from those who probably do not' (Last 1988: 118).

Now that we have defined screening, we need to explore how decisions are made about which problems to screen for.

Why did screening develop?

When initially introduced into health care, screening only really extended the therapeutic range. This was obviously based on the idea that the outcome could potentially be improved if a disease process could be identified and treatment started at an early stage. In diagrammatic terms this could be shown as:

(a) Without screening programme	(b) With screening programme
pathological changes	pathological changes
↓	↓
system presentation	screening
↓	↓
diagnosis	diagnosis
↓	↓
treatment	treatment

Note that there is a hoped for difference between (a) and (b) in the time from pathological changes occurring to treatment taking place.

Although screening continues to have the function of identifying pathological changes in at-risk individuals before symptoms present, it has also progressed to aim to prevent the onset of a disease altogether.

(c)	At risk of disease process
	↓
	screen
	↓
	prevent disease occurrence/action to reduce risk

An example of screening framework (b) would be cervical screening and an example of framework (c) would be genetic screening used in the pre-conceptual period. Try thinking of some more examples in Exercise 9.2.

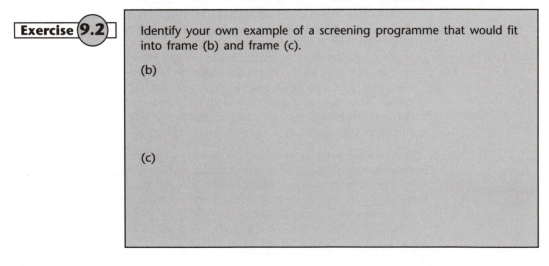

Exercise 9.2

Identify your own example of a screening programme that would fit into frame (b) and frame (c).

(b)

(c)

	Infant hearing	Cervical	PKU	BSE	Questionnaire
Once only			+		
Repeated		+		+	
Self				+	+
Opportunistic				+	
Universal	+		+		
Selective		+			
Time specific	+		+		

PKU: phenylketonuria
BSE: breast self-examination

Figure 9.1 Some different screening formats.

There are several different types of screening format. Some types of screening need to be carried out in a specific time scale. For example, phenyl-ketonuria (a hereditary enzyme deficiency) screening must be carried out shortly after birth, as severe mental deficiency would result if the diet was not amended immediately; the hearing distraction test for babies does not work effectively if the baby is much over 8–9 months. Other screening tests are not restricted to specific time scales and can be carried out opportunistically, i.e. whenever the opportunity presents. Some screening tests need to be carried out only once in a lifetime; others need to be repeated regularly. The whole population could potentially benefit from some screening programmes; others are targeted at a specific section of the population or one sex. Some examples of different screening formats are shown in Figure 9.1.

We have explored a definition of screening and identified some of the forms it can take. The next question to address is 'how are screening issues selected?' In other words, why do we only screen for some diseases and not all?

Consider the following statement: 'As long as sufficient finance is available, screening programmes should be established for every disease process.' Is it true or false?

The statement is false, because the development of a screening programme is not solely dependent on the availability of finance. Effective screening requires knowledge of the disease process as well as information on those at risk and the availability of effective treatment.

Screening criteria

Several criteria must be considered in any screening programme development. They may or may not all be met.

- there must be an identified need;
- the problem must present with sufficient frequency;
- it must be possible to identify those at risk;
- the test must be acceptable to the population at risk;
- the screening test must be reliable and valid;
- an acceptable and effective intervention must be available;
- the outcome for early intervention must be superior to that available when symptoms present naturally;
- the cost : benefit ratio must be acceptable.

We now need to explore some of the many issues involved in this list of screening criteria.

There must be an identified need

Usually, although not necessarily, this will be a disease process threatening individual and/or public health. For example, mass X-ray screening programmes were introduced in the 1940s when tuberculosis was a major threat to individual and public health, but were withdrawn in the 1980s when the threat of the disease had diminished.

There is an acceptable screening test

The test itself must have certain qualities, such as being easy to perform, which could reduce the possibility of tester error, acceptable financial cost and an acceptable experience for the individuals being screened. Consider the options in Exercise 9.3.

Consider how likely you would be to participate in a screening programme

(a) that involved providing a urine sample once per year at a local venue;

(b) that involved you undergoing sigmoidoscopy examination once per year.

Presumably the level of personal discomfort and inconvenience would be important factors. However, these considerations would no doubt be tempered by your perceived level of risk of actually suffering from a particular disease. We will develop these issues further later in the chapter.

An intervention strategy must be available

It would be totally unethical to develop and implement a screening test in order to identify a health problem for which there is no effective treatment strategy on offer.

The outcome for the disease is poor without early intervention

If there is an easy, cost-effective and successful treatment available for a disease it might be difficult to justify the professional, financial and personal investment involved in early identification through screening. It sounds straightforward common sense to say that screening should be used with diseases that have an improved outcome or prognosis as a consequence of early treatment. However, actually determining the benefits of early treatment is not as simple as it seems.

An important issue to clarify is exactly what we mean by improved outcome. All of the following might be seen as improved outcome:

- more people are cured of a particular disease;
- survival time is increased;
- extension of the length of time for which someone knows that he or she is suffering from an illness without an actual improvement in survival time.

Consider the following diagrams.

pathological changes	pathological changes
↓	↓
screen	system presentation
↓	↓
diagnosis	diagnosis
↓	↓
treat	treat
↓	↓
death	death

What has screening actually achieved?

What we are actually talking about here is 'lead time', which refers to the situation in which survival time *appears* to have improved simply because screening has led to the disease being diagnosed earlier that it would have presented by symptoms. You can see that assumptions about the effectiveness of screening can be complicated by using survival from time of diagnosis as a baseline measurement. This is not the only complicating factor when one is trying to determine the benefit of early diagnosis and treatment. For example, it may be that screening which takes place at three- or four-yearly intervals picks up a less aggressive form of a disease, e.g. cancer, than a cancer that presents symptomatically. Thus, again screening may *appear* to increase survival simply because screening is picking up less aggressive disease. We also need to give some thought to the individuals who present for screening: if the group who present have a higher incidence of the disease (e.g. the rates of cervical cancer and breast cancer are different in different social classes), then the identification and treatment rate would also be affected.

Targeting a screening programme

In view of the issues we have just discussed, it is clear that targeting of a screening programme is an important issue. Randomized controlled trials can provide information on the effectiveness of tests with different individuals, time scales for screening etc. We can use the example of mammography screening for breast cancer to demonstrate this. There is currently some debate about what age group of women to invite for screening and how often screening should take place. At the time of writing comparison of the outcome of screening for different age groups indicates that screening appears to reduce mortality from breast cancer for women aged 50–69, but the advantages to younger women are less clear.

The screening test itself must have certain qualities

Screening tests must be reliable; in other words, if the test is repeated on the same person the results should be consistent. The test must also be valid. Two measures of validity are sensitivity and specificity:

- test *sensitivity* is its ability to identify true positives, i.e. to identify disease that is actually present;
- test *specificity* is its ability to identify true negatives, i.e. when the test result says the disease is not present, it definitely is not present.

A screening test may have both high specificity and high sensitivity, the ideal situation. However, this is not always the case. Consider this further in Exercise 9.4.

Sensitivity and specificity determine how many true or false positives and negatives can be expected from a test.

What would be the situation with a test with high sensitivity but low specificity?

What about a test with high specificity and low sensitivity?

Which of the above two tests is preferable for screening?

A test with high sensitivity but low specificity would identify most of the people in a population with the disease, but would be less good at identifying those without the disease. In other words, there would be a large number of false positives – people who were positive on the test but did not actually have the disease. In a test with high specificity but low sensitivity the situation is reversed. The test is good at identifying those without the disease but less good at identifying those with the disease. There would be many false negatives – people negative on the test who do in fact have the disease. The ideal situation, of course, is to have a test which is highly sensitive and specific, but life is rarely like this. So if the choice is between high sensitivity and low specificity, and high specificity and low sensitivity, which is the best test? The answer is that it depends on the consequence of making the wrong decision. If the condition is worth screening for, then picking up all (or as near as possible) people who may have the disease, with those who don't being excluded by further tests, would seem the best option. However, a screening strategy based on a sensitive but not very specific test could become prohibitively expensive, in the sense of health care resources devoted to excluding the false positives, but also expensive to the false positives in terms of unnecessary worry that they may have a serious disease, and time, discomfort and possibly serious risk from further medical investigation.

There must be a strong likelihood that those at risk will participate in the screening offered

Even if a particular screening test is responding to a significant need, has acceptable levels of sensitivity and specificity and so on, unless it can be feasibly expected that those people at risk can be identified and contacted and will actually participate in screening, the programme would not be worthwhile or effective.

If the population at risk is in routine contact with the screener, then the screening has the potential for greater impact and efficiency. For example, all babies born in the UK are screened for phenylketonuria in hospital or by the community midwife; the screening programme virtually has a captive audience. When this type of screening is compared with a type that requires individuals to be selected and contacted to invite participation, the potential efficiency problems of the latter become apparent. Consider four scenarios in Exercise 9.5.

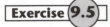

Exercise 9.5

Four examples of issues for which it may be appropriate to develop screening programmes are discussed below. Identify which screening criteria are present, which would not be met and any other information required to make a decision about screening for the particular problem.

Example 1

Tuberculosis continues to be a health problem, although treatment opportunities are generally good. Nearly half the notifications for the disease in England and Wales are migrants from countries with high incidence of TB. Consequently, migrants are forced to participate in screening at port health control units and their destination area is also informed to allow follow-up by community health personnel, e.g. health visitors.

Criteria:

Example 2

There have recently been considerable advances in gene location knowledge. It may consequently be possible to develop genetic screening programmes. However, assuming that some prioritization has to occur, should the screening be provided for the most severe forms of genetic disease or the most commonly occurring? There are numerous programmes under way to develop treatment programmes for various genetic diseases. Identifying the population that would benefit from screening may be a problem, as until people have children with a genetic problem they may not be aware that they are carriers.

Criteria:

Example 3

A primary health care team is concerned that the population it serves may be consuming unhealthy levels of alcohol. The team would like to identify those concerned to try to assist them to reduce their levels of alcohol consumption. They are considering opportunistic screening or mailing out a questionnaire.

Criteria:

Example 4

Some countries in Europe have started experimental screening for a certain type of cancer. This particular type of cancer has a poor prognosis with late diagnosis, although developments in treatment in recent years have shown some improvement. Economic constraints on research is often named as an inhibitor to further treatment development. If this screening programme is effective it could have a major impact on mortality from this disease, but results so far are not conclusive.

Criteria:

Compare your responses in Exercise 9.5 with the following suggestions. These responses are by no means complete, but raise some of the issues involved.

Example 1

- Significant number of at-risk individuals and public health risk.
- Migrants are an easily identifiable population.
- There is a valid test available to screen for the disease.
- The test is probably acceptable to those requiring screening.
- There is an effective treatment available for the disease.

Example 2

- It may be difficult to identify the target population.

- We have no details yet regarding the content of the screening test, and it would therefore be difficult to make judgements as to its acceptability.
- It is unclear whether we are to assume that the possible intervention is termination of pregnancy, or whether there is some other form of intervention and exactly what this would involve in personal and economic terms.
- In order to say whether the outcome from early intervention is superior we would have to become involved in value, ethical and religious judgement, e.g. in relation to learning disabilities.

More information is really required before any decisions about screening programmes could be made.

Example 3

- The team appears to have identified a need, although it only appears to be at the level of assumptions.
- The test the team seems to have in mind is one of questioning individuals about their alcohol consumption, either in person or by questionnaire. Some people may want to participate in this and others may not.
- It would be difficult to verify the accuracy of the responses received.
- The effectiveness of a health promotion strategy to address alcohol consumption is not certain.

Example 4

- The outcome of treatment is improved with early diagnosis and treatment.
- We are uncertain as to whether the screening test is reliable or valid. There is obviously an ethical dilemma that if the screening turns out to be successful and we have not implemented it until after the experimental period, many lives could have been saved.

One of the screening criteria we have identified is that of the test being acceptable to those at risk. Another major factor to consider in any discussion on screening is participation. It does not necessarily follow that at-risk groups will participate in a screening programme available to them.

Why do individuals participate in screening?

Start to answer the question by asking yourself why you have participated or why you would ever consider participating in screening.

People may participate in screening to be reassured that they are healthy, or to discover that they have a health problem. The former motive is probably the stronger. In order to expose yourself deliberately to the knowledge that your health is under threat you must:

- be aware of your risk;
- consider the risk to be sufficiently great;
- have confidence that there is an acceptable treatment available to you;
- find the screening procedure sufficiently accessible and acceptable.

Experience and research have identified several factors that appear to influence participation in screening. Gender seems to be an important factor, in that men seem more reluctant than women to attend, but it is also more likely that women will be in contact with health care professionals perhaps because of family planning or child care needs. Attenders and non-attenders seem to hold different beliefs about control and fatalism with respect to health. Other apparently significant factors include level of education, age, marital status and number of dependants. Martin and Main (see Further Reading) consider the influence of health belief models on participation in cervical cancer screening. Knowledge of these factors should help health care workers to use the most appropriate means of inviting participation for different client groups.

This discussion on participation must also include the question: 'is or should participation in screening be a free choice?' Should it always be up to the individual to decide whether to participate or should any level of pressure be exerted? If it is more cost-effective for society in general to treat a disease at an early stage (in terms of health care costs, sick leave costs etc.), should individuals be allowed free choice in participation? Consider this in Exercise 9.6.

 **Exercise 9.6**

Consider the following examples and make some judgement as to the level of free choice that should be available. There are no right or wrong answers, this is an opportunity for you to consider some of the emotions, ethics and complexities involved.

How much choice should parents be allowed in participating in developmental screening for their children or infant hearing screening?

What level of persuasion should be used for women to attend for cervical screening? What happens in your area when women fail to attend? Are they offered a repeat invitation; does a health visitor make a home visit; does the GP attempt to persuade the individual the next time she attends the surgery, even for an unrelated issue?

What is assumed to be the most responsible action of a pregnant woman who is at high risk of passing a genetic disease to her child, assuming there is screening available for that particular disease?

Is it reasonable to expect a 39-year-old mother expecting her first child to undertake amniocentesis screening for Down's Syndrome, especially as the only 'cure' to a positive result is termination of pregnancy?

Summary

Working through the chapter should have helped you to answer the questions posed at the beginning. You can use the following headings to summarize the most important aspects of the chapter for you.

1 Give a definition of screening.

2 What are the principles guiding decisions about why we screen for some diseases and not others?

3 Drawing on your knowledge of why people do or do not participate in screening, list four reasons why a screening programme may have a high participation rate:

(a)

(b)

(c)

(d)

List four reasons why a screening programme may have a low participation rate:

(a)

(b)

(c)

(d)

You may wish to investigate these issues further, and if so you could collect information about the uptake rates of national or local screening programmes and suggest some explanations for the rates.

CHAPTER 10

THE EFFECTIVENESS OF HEALTH CARE: A HISTORICAL PERSPECTIVE

How do efficacy, effectiveness and efficiency differ?

How effective was health care in the past?

How effective was public health in the past?

After working through this chapter you should be able to:

- define common terms used in assessing health care;

- discuss why clinical medicine and doctors enjoyed high status in the nineteenth century, despite the fact that many of the remedies used were ineffective or harmful;

- give examples of efficacious public health activities in the nineteenth century;

- discuss why, historically, public health was often attacked, and its efficacious measures resisted.

Why did health improve in Europe over the past 200 years?

Many people, perhaps particularly those involved in health care such as nurses and doctors, have long tended to assume that health care must save lives. They believe that the fall in death rates over the past two centuries in Europe must have been owing to the impressive growth of medical knowledge during that period. It is only during recent decades that systematic investigations of past patterns of health compared with medical practices at the time have led to this assumption being called into question. Most of the fall in mortality was owing to reductions in deaths from communicable diseases and these occurred before any specific treatments or preventive techniques were available (except for smallpox). McKeown (see Further Reading) argued that greater host resistance because of better average nutrition was the major factor, although he was aware of the important contribution of sanitary improvements (such as the provision of clean water) in reducing deaths from waterborne diseases. There have been disagreements about some aspects of his arguments, but his main thesis, that clinical advances could not have been the main factors in improving health statistics, stands. This does not mean, though, that health care interventions had no beneficial effects. To judge that, we need to examine what their intended purposes were. We will also consider who the practitioners of the past were, and what they did. We will then repeat the process for public health.

Definitions

First, we need to understand some terms that are commonly used in evaluating health activities. They are *efficacy*, *effectiveness* and *efficiency*. These are related, but they are not the same.

- *Efficacy* refers to the extent to which a health care intervention produces a beneficial result under ideal conditions. 'Ideal conditions' often means under the conditions in a study set up to find out if the intervention has the desired effect. The resources put into implementing the intervention in a study may far exceed those which can be used when the intervention is implemented more widely, such as part of a general health service.
- *Effectiveness* refers to the extent to which a health care intervention does what it is intended to do when delivered under everyday conditions.
- *Efficiency* of a health care intervention refers to the end results achieved in relation to the money, resources and time put into the intervention. These 'end results' are often not defined in terms of effectiveness, but may be more to do with providing a particular service. An 'efficient service' could refer to one provided at low cost, irrespective of its effectiveness.
- *Cost-effectiveness* considers both the benefit gained and the costs of achieving it. If two procedures with different costs give the same benefit, then using the cheaper one would free up resources to tackle other problems, and could be described as more cost-effective.

The purpose of clinical practice and health interventions

Unless we know what we are trying to achieve, we cannot begin to study whether we are achieving it.

The healer's tasks have been summarized as 'to cure sometimes, to relieve often and to comfort always'. A further injunction is that the healer should do no harm. To be able to assess effectiveness, then, we need evidence that no harm was done, and that some or all of cure, relief and comfort was achieved. As we shall see, such evidence is sparse, especially for the past.

Who were the practitioners of the past, taking Britain as an example?

From earliest recorded history, there have been people who took a special interest in the healing arts and midwifery. Often it was senior women in a community who did this, having learned from their mothers and from experience. They would be called on to diagnose, to tend the sick, to advise, to prescribe, prepare and administer herbs and to help women in labour. Their roles thus included both 'medical' and 'nursing' functions. As society became more complex, more specialization developed, and by medieval times we find many sorts of healers. There were physicians, who were gentlemen with a university education who served the elite, while apothecaries and barber surgeons who had served apprenticeships were mostly at the service of the middle classes. Nursing in hospitals was usually done by members of religious orders. Most ordinary folk still called on local wise women (and some men) when they needed care or advice.

In the middle of the nineteenth century, after a long campaign by the organizations of the physicians, surgeons and apothecaries, medicine became a unified 'profession'. This means that only members of the profession could claim to be doctors. To become a doctor, examinations had to be passed, and names entered on the Medical Register, training and entry to the profession being very much under the control of its members. (The men took this opportunity to exclude women altogether from doctoring.) At the same time, Florence Nightingale had set out to raise the standards and status of nursing, which, as secular hospitals had increased, had become the province of servants and inmates. She succeeded in establishing nurse training, but it was another 60 years before nurse registration was achieved, long after the midwives in 1902. Meanwhile, many patients in charitable and public institutions did not have trained nurses to care for them.

The doctors succeeded because they were able to persuade legislators and others that they alone were masters of an esoteric body of knowledge which gave them the capacity to heal. Others, without being trained in such knowledge, were unfit to be allowed to be healers. In other words, decision makers have been convinced that these doctors were effective. What was the evidence?

How effective were doctors and other health carers in the nineteenth and early twentieth centuries?

In 1850 there were some efficacious remedies, mostly herbal medicines, of which many were also used by the village wise women. These could give relief if not cure. Examples were digitalis (fox glove) for heart failure and opiates (from poppies) for pain. Doctors also had and used other powerful drugs, such as those which caused purging and vomiting, and they freely prescribed bleeding and leeches for all sorts of conditions. Present knowledge suggests that many of these common prescriptions and practices were generally not only useless but positively dangerous. Surgeons had a limited repertoire, largely concerned with emergencies. Since they had no anaesthetics, patients were plied with alcohol and then held down by strong men while the surgeon used his strength and speed to, for example, saw off a gangrenous leg.

Medical knowledge was growing all the time, but even when of direct relevance to practice was often slow to be applied. For example, Semmelweiss in Vienna and Wendell Holmes in Boston recognized that childbed fever occurred more commonly on the wards where students attended deliveries, and realized that 'contagion' was being carried from the post mortem room to the labouring women. In their hospitals, cross-infection was reduced by making the students wash their hands, but it was many years before most institutions changed their practices. Generally, men midwives attending childbirth, like surgeons, still did not wash their hands or change out of their frockcoats even if they were applying forceps. It was not surprising that, as Florence Nightingale estimated, institutional maternal mortality in the mid-nineteenth century was seven times higher than in home deliveries, and so it long remained.

Throughout the nineteenth century, cross-infection remained rife on surgical and fever wards too, and at that time it could not be claimed that hospital care, in general, did the patient no harm. Later, as Nightingale's trained nurses began to appear on some wards, and as bacteriology and the idea of cross-infection began to be more fashionable, some hospitals gradually became less hazardous places.

In the 1860s, Lister introduced antisepsis into surgery, having theatres sprayed with carbolic acid, and when ether and chloroform began to be used as anaesthetic agents, surgery started to be safer and wider in scope. Asepsis – using sterile instruments in a sterile environment – had to wait until the twentieth century. In the 1930s cross-matching of blood was developed, and then relaxant and other anaesthetic agents were introduced and surgery began to look like something we would recognize today.

There were some medical developments, too. For example, early in the twentieth century vitamins were identified and their use in the prevention and treatment of deficiency diseases was recognized, although vitamin deficiency diseases remained common in the United Kingdom until the Second World War. In the 1920s insulin treatment for diabetes was developed. As we have seen, the big killers of the nineteenth century were infectious diseases, and the first synthetic drugs to treat infections were not developed until the very end of the century, when arsenicals and mercury were first used in the treatment of syphilis. It was not until 1935 that the first drugs active against common bacterial infections were produced, the sulphonamides, followed later by penicillin and streptomycin, the first of many antibiotics. It was then that medical treatment became able to make a significant difference to the chance of surviving some serious infections.

Now see if in Exercise 10.1 you can give any answers to the question: 'how effective were doctors and other health carers in the mid-nineteenth and early twentieth century?'

Exercise 10.1

Sum up from reading so far your impression of how effective doctors and other health carers were in the mid-nineteenth and early twentieth centuries. Consider your responses under the three purposes of health interventions: to cure, to relieve and to comfort, all guided by the maxim 'first do no harm'.

In Exercise 10.1 you probably mentioned that there were few cures but some efficacious remedies which gave benefit by relieving symptoms. There were also other efficient treatments, in that they could be relied on to cause vomiting, purging and bleeding as intended, but which are now seen as giving overall physical disbenefit and so certainly were not effective in enhancing health. What about comfort? Did the doctors provide this? Probably yes. The feeling that a knowledgeable person has taken your case in hand implies that everything possible will be done to help you. Even if the treatment involves disastrous procedures like repeated bleeding, you gain comfort, in the sense of reassurance, from the doctor's care, and so do your family and friends. Nightingale's nurses were taught to attend to all aspects of the comfort of their patients, and they, and informed lay carers, probably saw 'making the patient comfortable' as their most important task.

Doctors, then, could rarely cure, but could provide some relief and comfort to patients. What we do not know is how often they did this effectively, although we do know they used harmful treatments. We also do not know what proportion of the sick population were cared for by doctors or trained nurses, so we can make no estimate of how effectively relief and comfort was provided at the population level. We can be fairly confident, though, that in the absence of efficacious curative remedies, doctors could have contributed little to falling death rates.

As we have seen, despite these shortcomings, the standing of doctors was so high in 1859 that they were accorded in Britain the monopoly on healing. A combination of factors contributed to what now appears to be the quite unwarranted status given to doctors. The ability to relieve and comfort was valued, and the growth of medical knowledge commanded admiration even though it was slow to have any impact. However, almost certainly people also believed that doctors did cure them. The reason for this lies largely in the natural history of diseases. Most diseases, in most people, most of the time, are cured by nature. However, if any healer is consulted in the course of the illness, he or she may be credited with the cure. Conversely, some diseases are usually fatal and a skilled healer will recognize this and warn of the likely outcome, and again accept the credit for the few who do recover.

The story of public health is very different. We now turn to that.

Purposes of public health

Once again, we need to ask what it is for. What is the purpose of public health activities?

Public health is concerned with the health of populations and in this section we are looking in particular at protecting health and preventing disease. This is called primary prevention and can be considered the equivalent of curative activities in clinical medicine. Public health, like clinical practice, has the obligation of doing more good than harm for the population as a whole. This proves to be a difficult concept when looked at from the individual point of view. Consider, for example, a child being immunized against diphtheria. The child is almost sure to get a sore arm and perhaps other discomforts as a direct result of the immunization. However, when the child does not get diphtheria, no one can say this is a benefit of the immunization – he or she may not have caught diphtheria anyway. What you can say is that mass immunization of children has been shown to reduce diphtheria infection rates greatly, and thus to reduce everyone's chance of infection and benefit the community as a whole. The disbenefits to individuals are balanced by benefits to all.

Who were our public health predecessors?

Since written records began, there have always been doctors who have taken an interest in public health issues, though these doctors have probably been in a minority in the profession. Often they practised clinical medicine too, although when in Britain medical officers of health were appointed in the late nineteenth century, they often became full-timers, to avoid conflicts of interest. However, doctors have never been the only people with such an interest. Social reformers and nurses, including Nightingale, politicians, national and local government officers and others, have always been involved, indeed often in the lead.

In Britain, probably the most influential name in public health reform in the nineteenth century was that of Edwin Chadwick, a lawyer by training. He served on many government commissions investigating social problems, and his first interest was controlling pauperism, becoming the main architect of the hated 1834 Poor Law. However, he came to recognize that ill health was a major cause of pauperism and he became obsessed with what he called the 'sanitary idea'. He set out to demonstrate that living conditions, particularly in the industrial towns, gave rise to appalling levels of ill health, compiling a detailed and influential report for the Poor Law Commissioners, the *Sanitary Condition of the Working Population of Great Britain*. The first effective public health legislation was based on recommendations of this report, establishing a national General Board of Health. He took on opposed vested interests to fight for the setting up of appropriate legislative and administrative structures, with national standards laid down to be implemented by local government. Amazingly, he also put forward a practical engineering solution to the problem of insanitary towns:

an arterial water circulation system which used small bore pipes to carry clean water in and other small bore pipes to remove waste and sewage.

In the second half of the nineteenth century in the UK, the public health function became one of the duties of local government. Medical officers of health were appointed as senior local government officers with large departments. From this powerful position they were able to use their professional expertise and standing to advise, advocate, plan and, when their councils agreed, implement measures to improve the living conditions and health of the local population. The frontline staff of the medical officers of health were the sanitary inspectors, but the medical officers of health also had much to do. In large authorities they later came to carry administrative responsibilities for the growing number of hospital and other care services which local authorities should or could provide, and then for a wide range of maternal and child health and expanded school health services. At this stage, early in the twentieth century, a growing number of midwives, community nurses and clinical medical officers – public health clinicians – joined public health departments.

In summary, public health has never been a medical monopoly. It has overlapped and does overlap with clinical tasks in individual prevention, but its fixed point is a focus on the whole community and what seems necessary to improve the health of that community.

How effective has public health activity been in promoting health and preventing disease?

Before we address this question, let us look again at the other side of the balance sheet: possible disbenefits caused by public health activity. This, as we have seen, is perhaps even more difficult than in the case of comparing benefit and disbenefit from a clinical procedure, because it may be difficult to know which particular individuals have benefited, and some individuals may have serious disbenefits, even if the overall benefit for the whole community is great. In Exercise 10.2 list the potential disbenefits of public health activity that you can think of.

Exercise 10.2

What harmful effects might public health activity have? Think broadly and include harmful health effects to individuals and populations, and include non-health effects, such as effects on personal liberty.

We have already looked at an immunization programme in the context of harmful effects, but a stronger example might be closing down a vendor of contaminated food. Not every customer would have become ill, so you cannot say who benefited, and the vendor may go out of business. But a serious outbreak of salmonella food poisoning may have been averted, avoiding the risk of deaths, secondary spread, many people off work and considerable cost to individuals, firms and the health service.

Some past public health activities were inadequate. For example, cellar dwellings were compulsorily closed because they were insanitary. But no powers existed at that time for housing to be built for those rendered homeless, so the remaining local housing, marginally better than the cellars, became even more overcrowded. Other activities were probably useless and certainly caused great distress, but were no doubt done, like many treatments, because something had to be done, and people had persuaded themselves that it was beneficial. Much quarantine and isolation must have fallen in that category, although isolation of smallpox patients was probably of benefit to the community.

Scientific experiments to test the benefit of public health activities are even more difficult to carry out than those to test individual treatments, for many reasons, including that large numbers and long time scales may be required.

Let us now look at three examples of effective public health measures.

Smallpox prevention

Smallpox was a well known killer in medieval times and before. A preventive measure called variolation was known to the Chinese 3000 years ago. This involved scratching matter from the scab of a smallpox patient into another's arm. This usually resulted in a mild attack of smallpox and subsequent immunity, but it could kill the variolated person and could spread to other contacts. Probably it was adopted only because smallpox was regarded as sure to infect almost everyone, and to kill many if acquired naturally. The procedure was introduced into England from Turkey in 1717 by the wife of a former British ambassador to Turkey. It became widely used and is believed to have led to a fall in mortality from smallpox.

At the end of the eighteenth century, Jenner, an English country doctor, noted that milkmaids had good complexions, rarely being marked by smallpox scars. He listened to their own explanation, which was that they did not catch smallpox because they had already had the cowpox, and he carried out an experiment to test this. He showed that by scratching material from a cowpox into the arm, a child could be protected from subsequent infection by variolation. This was probably the first example of artificially and safely creating immunity by what came to be called vaccination. This measure was efficacious but it did not quickly become effective because it was many years before the procedure was widely used. The vaccine was made available free from the 1840s but it was not until vaccination was made compulsory, that most children in Britain were protected.

The delay in giving protection to the whole world by eradicating small-pox took even longer. In 1966, when the WHO committed itself and its funds to eradication, the disease was still endemic in 30 countries. It took an enormous concerted effort over years before, in 1980, the WHO was confident that the world could be declared free of smallpox.

Scurvy

Scurvy, which we now know is caused by vitamin C deficiency, has a long history as a scourge on the high seas. At the end of the sixteenth century it was known to have been the greatest killer of sailors on long voyages since the earliest days of the great navigators a hundred years before. This was despite knowledge of folk medicines in several parts of the world to prevent and cure it, e.g. by an infusion of pine needles.

In 1601, James Lancaster, who was responsible for victualling four ships of the East India Company bound for India, decided to give lemon juice every day to the sailors on the biggest ship. Few of these became ill or died, in contrast to the situation on the smaller ships, where a third of the men died. Unfortunately, this finding did not lead to future sailors being protected. A century and a half later, in 1747, James Lind, a naval physi-cian who knew of Lancaster's work, compared citrus fruit with various other treatments for 12 sailors with scurvy. The two who received two oranges and one lemon daily quickly recovered, unlike the others, but it took another half century before, in 1795, the British Navy introduced citrus fruit as a routine preventive measure into sailors' diets. The Merchant Navy did not do the same until 1865.

Diphtheria

A more recent example of delayed benefit to public health is diphtheria vaccination. The bacterium causing diphtheria was identified in 1883 and antitoxin treatment became available in 1895, for use in treatment. How-ever, the big breakthrough was when immunization became possible in 1913, and subsequent reliable research showed that it was effective in pro-tecting a large proportion of the children immunized against infection. The government's chief medical officer advocated universal child immun-ization in 1922, but 3000 children died every year until the wartime ethos that planning and managing for the health of the nation was a priority led to action. A national immunization campaign was launched in 1942, virtually eliminating diphtheria in the United Kingdom.

Overview

Do you think that the evidence given supports the view that Chadwick's small bore sanitation system, vaccination against smallpox, citrus fruit to prevent scurvy and diphtheria immunization were efficacious meas-ures? If you think that some or all of them were efficacious, why was their implementation opposed and/or delayed? One can observe that evidence of efficacy is not necessarily enough to promote change, and as is addressed in Chapter 11, this is just as true today as it was in the past.

In Chadwick's case a powerful alliance of vested interests grew up against him. Some just did not like him or resented a mere lawyer poking his nose into medical matters, but others felt they stood to lose a lot. Corrupt local government did not want central government instruction and inspection, and feared the loss of power. Those who profited from the causes of ill health had most to lose. The slum landlord, the company supplying polluted water, the employer of child labour in mine, factory and mill, the industrial polluter, the vendor of polluted food could see no case for disturbing the status quo. They pleaded freedom of trade, public demand, creating employment, competition from elsewhere, if we don't others will do and so on. Public health is still all too familiar with these kind of arguments.

It is less easy to see who stood to gain from failure to prevent smallpox, scurvy or diphtheria, and perhaps the explanation owed more to cock-up than conspiracy. There were no effective mechanisms to carry out the preventive measures, it was no one's responsibility to make things happen, people who could have done something did not have the necessary information, it would have cost money, there was no demand for it. All these factors too have almost always stood in the way of public health innovations alongside the threatened vested interests.

Public health initiatives on balance were effective in contributing to the improvement of population health in the past two centuries, but not nearly as effective as they could have been. The lessons from the past are just as relevant today. Public health practitioners of whatever background need not only efficacious measures, but also social, political and managerial skills and many allies, if the best results are to be obtained and effectiveness is to be improved.

Summary

Write your own summary of this chapter by answering the questions below.

1 Define and contrast the terms efficacy, effectiveness and efficiency.

2 Discuss the reasons for the high status of clinical medicine in the nineteenth century despite the lack of evidence for its effectiveness.

3 Give examples of efficacious preventive measures which did contribute to or could have contributed to improvements in population health in the nineteenth century.

4 Describe some of the problems which faced public health advocates in the nineteenth century.

5 What lessons do you think can be learnt for public health practice today from examining the role of public health over the past 200 years? (Think broadly, e.g. relative status given to public health versus clinical care, opposing vested interests, building alliances.)

CHAPTER 11

ASSESSING THE EFFECTIVENESS OF HEALTH CARE TODAY

How can we know if treatment and prevention services are effective?

What are the characteristics of an effective treatment or prevention service and what information can be obtained about these?

Why is information on service effectiveness often ignored and why are ineffective services delivered?

After working through this chapter you should be able to:

• outline the characteristics of an effective health service;

• describe approaches to evaluating health service effectiveness;

• discuss the strengths and weaknesses of different kinds of health service information;

• discuss the reasons why evidence on health service effectiveness is often ignored by those providing health services, and how this may be remedied.

How effective are treatment and preventive services today?

You may have been surprised to learn in Chapters 6 and 10 that health care had limited effects on health in the past. You may be even more suprised to find that some people claim that the same applies today. Some critics, like Ivan Illich, go further and argue that medicine is the cause of many modern ills. He gets some backing from the findings of medical sociologists who have examined people's experiences in receiving health care, and found that these can sometimes be damaging and devaluing, particularly to disadvantaged group members, such as women and people from ethnic minorities. From within the ranks of health workers too there have been some disturbing criticisms, based on the lack of objective evidence of benefit from many health service activities, and wide variations in how particular health problems are dealt with by different professionals. On the other hand, as every TV viewer knows, 'medical breakthroughs' occur every week. It is time for us to investigate! We will look first at treatments, then at treatment services, and then move on to prevention.

There can be no doubt that many modern treatments can be beneficial. Reflect on some that you are aware of in Exercise 11.1

**Exercise 11.1**

List some examples you know of efficacious treatments which have become available in the past 50 years.

You may have mentioned drugs like streptomycin and its successors for treating tuberculosis, and antibiotics which save some lives and shorten the course of many infections. Other drugs can now cure some malignant diseases, like some childhood leukaemias. There have been many developments in surgery too, including transplant surgery and joint replacements, and no doubt you thought of many other treatments.

However many you thought of, though, these would be only a tiny proportion of the new treatments introduced in the past 50 years, some of which have come and gone, and others of which are still in use. For many of them, and indeed for older treatments still used, objective evidence that they work, and work better than alternatives for the problems they are used for, is often lacking.

Efficacy and effectiveness

Before we go further it is important to note the distinction (also made in Chapter 10) between efficacy and effectiveness. *Efficacy* refers to the extent to which a specific intervention, such as a treatment for a disease, produces a beneficial result under ideal conditions. 'Ideal conditions' usually means in a carefully conducted study. *Effectiveness* is the extent to which an intervention produces the desired beneficial result under 'everyday' conditions. Thus, to be effective a health service must deliver interventions known to be efficacious, but more than this it must do so to a high enough standard that the intervention, known to be beneficial under ideal conditions, remains so when delivered as a service.

Approaches to measuring efficacy were covered in Chapter 4. The gold standard is the randomized controlled trial (although for practical reasons not all interventions can be covered in this way). Many of the randomized controlled trials carried out are only able to include a relatively small number of patients, and the results obtained could have been owing to chance. Two such apparently similar trials may give opposite results, and clinical workers, faced with more and more publications to read, may not be aware of or feel able to interpret the meaning of several different trials of the same treatments. Recently, the technique of *meta-analysis* has begun to be more widely used. This is the process, using statistical methods, by which the results of several studies can be combined. Thus, for a particular intervention or treatment it is possible to pull together the results from all reliable trials, published and unpublished, to allow conclusions to be reached based on larger numbers. The Cochrane Collaboration, originating in Oxford, England, is facilitating the collaboration of workers in many parts of the world to review research in their areas of interest, subject it to review and meta-analysis and make the results widely known. Slowly, health workers will be able to base more and more of their daily work on the best scientific evidence available.

We may look forward to a future in which health worker and client should be able to sit together by a computer and, based on the client's needs, produce an appropriateness rating for the treatment options available. From such a sequence, informed decisions could be reached and informed consent given, making full use of the present state of knowledge. By no means all of even the common treatments have been subject to enough reliable research for such a scenario to be possible yet. In many cases, there is an urgent need for the research to be done, but meanwhile health care team members will have to offer advice on treatment as best they can. Buckman and Lewith (see Further Reading) have suggested that every consulting room should carry a notice saying something like 'the doctor may recommend drugs which have not yet been proved to have a specific action against diseases. However, they are believed to be safe, some patients find them beneficial and they may help you.' A similar notice could be used by surgeons and most other health care workers, and might promote greater openness and mutual understanding in consultations.

Assessing the effectiveness of treatment services

As indicated above, the overall impact on health of a health service depends on more than the efficacy of the treatments it uses. We have seen that assessing treatments is not simple, and assessing services is even more complex. To make it more manageable it is usual to consider parts of a service such as those concerned with sufferers from a particular disease or group of diseases.

Service effectiveness can be considered from two angles: the effectiveness of the service for those who use it, and its effectiveness in meeting the needs of all those in the catchment population who could benefit from the service. We will try to keep both angles in mind. To start considering some of the components of service effectiveness, have a look at Exercise 11.2.

> You have been asked to assess the effectiveness of a particular service for children. The service is based in an inner-city area. Assuming that the treatment being offered by the service is known to be efficacious, list some things you would like to know about the service to help you judge whether it is effective in delivering the treatment.

The things you mention should fall under one or more of the following headings: four As and B, C, D and E. These stand for:

- *Available, Accessible, Acceptable, Appropriate*;
- delivery in the *Best* way;
- *Concentrated* where the need is greatest;
- *Delivering* what it sets out to deliver;
- committed to *Evaluation* of its impact on levels of health.

We can illustrate these by thinking about what effectiveness would mean for the service in Exercise 11.2. The service would be generally *available*, with flexible hours and short waiting lists, and known to be available by the local population. It would be easily *accessible*, by walking or public transport from the inner city, and would have parking space and facilities for wheelchairs and pushchairs. The clinic arrangements would be *acceptable* to grown-ups and children, with a pleasant environment providing play areas, changing areas and refreshments. To be *appropriate*, it would have staff who spoke local minority languages, and spoken and written communications would be understandable to parents and children, and cover all the points they want to know about.

Consideration would be given to how the service would be *best* provided. Would it need to see people in hospital outpatient departments or could it be provided in primary care or clinic settings? Would shared care involving both specialist and generalist doctors and nurses be appropriate? Resources should be *concentrated* on inner-city areas. The service should have a way of monitoring its *delivery*, making sure it was reaching all who need it, not just the most articulate regular attenders.

Evaluation would include attempts to measure the impact of the service on the physical, mental and social health of the child patients and their families, and to estimate what proportion of all the children in the area who would benefit from the service were actually using it.

Types of information available and required to evaluate treatment service effectiveness

One way of categorizing health service information is to put it under one of three headings: input, process or outcomes.

- *input* means the resources committed to the service;
- *process* is about the activities carried out with the resources;
- *outcomes* are the results of these service activities.

Consider these headings in more detail in Exercise 11.3

Exercise 11.3

> Consider again the service for children used in Exercise 11.2. Write down the items of information on the service you put under each of the headings.
>
> Input:
>
>
>
>
>
> Process:
>
>
>
>
>
> Outcomes:

Under each of these headings are included quantitative aspects (how much?) and qualitative aspects (how good?), but most of the routine information is about quantity not quality.

Under *input* you could have included the money spent on the service and its various parts, and what the money was spent on, such as x nurses, y doctors, z other staff, overheads of buildings, consumables like X-rays and dressings etc. All of these should be available, with some quality data, such as qualifications held by professional staff.

The *process* heading includes most of the data usually routinely available on health service activity, such as number of inpatient admissions, occupied bed-days, average length of stay, outpatient attendances and operations carried out. (It should be noted these usually refer to events, not individuals, so that 100 inpatient admissions could be 100 different patients admitted, or one patient admitted 100 times, or 50 patients admitted under one consultant and transferred to another, or any combination.) An example of a quality process indicator would be time spent on an inpatient waiting list.

Outcomes are what we really want to know: what gains in health result from the activities of this service? You will not be surprised that the answer is not available from routine data. The question is complex, comparable to asking about the efficacy of a treatment, and demands special studies. Nevertheless, governments and other funders of health care are keen to have 'outcome league tables' and have tried to construct these, often without adequate precautions to ensure that like is being compared with like. In Exercise 11.4 identify some of the difficulties in comparing outcomes between different providers of health care.

Exercise 11.4

You hear on the local news programme that one of the two hospitals in the area has a higher case fatality rate in surgical operations than the other hospital. The journalist is keen to conclude that this means the care is worse in the hospital with the higher rate. What else would you like to know before accepting this conclusion?

Probably you recalled that in Chapter 6 we discovered that there are many determinants of life and death apart from health care. A hospital serving a deprived ageing community, even with an excellent surgical service, would be likely to get worse results than one serving a younger affluent community. Allowance could be made for age profile and case mix, but the general health of the population and the prevalence of other problems like industrial lung disease, the stage of illness at which they reached hospital, their state of nutrition and many other factors would make profound differences to the chances of survival too. Of course, if a majority of the patients operated on in one hospital died, and *none* in another, this would look suspicious, but there may be a simple explanation. The no-deaths hospital may discharge all poorly patients post-operatively to a terminal care facility elsewhere.

Most of the information we have discussed so far for assessing the effectiveness of health care has been to do with quantity and not quality. Meaningful data on quality are not routinely available, and special studies are required. For example, instruments for recording the perceived quality of life of patients after using a service have been developed, and many outcome studies will be incomplete unless they include this dimension, which is after all the bottom line in any reckoning of the effectiveness of a service. Are the patients' lives as good as they could possibly be, after they have used the service?

Finally, a health service may be delivering an effective quality service from the point of view of its users, but may be failing to be effective from the population perspective. One can talk about the effectiveness of a service from the point of view of its users, and about the *community effectiveness* of the service from the point of view of the population the health service serves. Community effectiveness refers to the impact the service has on the whole community. For a service to be effective on the population level, it must cover a high proportion of all those in the population with the health problem for which the service was designed. Effectively treating a few per cent of the people with the condition will make little impact on the community as a whole. Evaluation of community effectiveness requires the same information already discussed to assess the effectiveness of the service from the point of view of the people using it, *and* it requires information on the proportion of people within the community who could benefit from the service who are actually using it.

In summary, in most health services, data routinely collected have not been designed for the purpose of assessing effectiveness. In the British National Health Service the main thrust has been on documenting quantities of activity, although in the market era introduced in the late 1980s efforts have been made to link these to input data, so that costs can be assigned to the activities. Some first attempts have been made to measure the quality of the activities, although many aspects of quality are not yet covered. Reliable data on outcomes are not available and probably could not be collected routinely at a reasonable cost.

Assessing the effectiveness of primary prevention measures

Primary prevention, the prevention of disease or other health problems arising, covers a very broad range of activities carried out by an equally broad range of people and organizations. Measures include immunization programmes, fluoridation of water to prevent dental caries, smoking prevention and road safety legislation. As with treatment services, there are two components to be considered: the efficacy of the interventions available and the effectiveness in delivering them.

The measures our public health predecessors installed in the industrialized world, such as clean water piped to every home, decent housing and controls on food safety and air pollution, are probably among the most efficacious measures there will ever be. At the end of the twentieth century, the public health agenda still has to include the vigorous support of all these areas. They are still lacking in many parts of the world and where they exist some are under serious threat, while others face new sorts of challenges.

As far as new measures are concerned, we need to pay particular attention to the benefit : disbenefit ratio at the population level before widespread introduction. Since, as we saw in Chapter 6, so many health problems have multiple causes, and many 'causes' result in many different problems, a range of preventive approaches has to be tried. Evaluation often presents difficulties, because the desired outcomes may be in the distant future, and other determinants may also be operating, negating benefit. This makes it all the more important that careful studies of new measures are done early on. Ideally, these should have a control group, and they must be able to identify and measure disbenefits and where necessary specify intermediate outcomes that can be measured in the time scale of the study. Randomized controlled trials are the gold standard for measuring the efficacy of many preventive measures, just as they are for treatment evaluations. Many preventive interventions are better implemented on a population or community level rather than an individual level. These can be evaluated in community intervention trials in which whole communities are randomized to receive the intervention or not. These are discussed briefly in Chapter 4.

What should be considered in the assessment of the effectiveness of prevention services? One approach would be to argue, as the British health departments did in 1976, that prevention and health are everyone's business. It would follow that all sorts of agencies, from government departments downwards, and almost everyone who works in health care should be engaged in the prevention business, and therefore that what they actually do for prevention should be assessed. That certainly ought to be done, but for practical reasons this section will focus on those health services particularly involved in prevention.

The criteria used in the assessment of treatment services (four As, B, C, D, E) can also be applied to the evaluation of preventive services. Pressure of illness may force people to use treatment services even if they don't like them. They have no such pressure to use preventive services if they do not meet the four As quality criteria. To be able to meet these criteria, providers of preventive services for individuals need to have registers with full, accurate and up-to-date details of their target groups. Then they are able to inform them individually that the service is *available* and to invite them personally, at the right time, to come to the service; for example, for immunization. The language of the invitation, verbal or written, must be *appropriate*. Choice should be offered of *accessible* and convenient locations and appointment times. The service must record whether they come or not and follow up if they do not, at the same time checking whether the service is failing to be *acceptable* in some way.

Effective prevention requires priority being given to those who have the greatest difficulty in improving their health, so *best* models, *concentration* on targets and *delivery* where needed are crucial. There is still much to be learned about promoting prevention in communities with the worst health, so innovations are called for, and these innovations must be *evaluated* so that good results can be disseminated.

Activities included under health promotion which target communities rather than specific individuals also need to meet these criteria, although they are often much more difficult to characterize.

Types of information available and required to evaluate preventive activities

For *individual preventive measures*, data comparable to those for treatment services may be available:

- *Input data.* For example, in the UK the resources committed to community health services, which are largely preventive, can be obtained, although the resources committed to prevention by general (family) practitioner services may be difficult to calculate. Some staffing data, such as health visitors employed per 1000 births, may also be available.
- *Process.* These include clinic sessions held and home visits and school visits carried out for preventive purposes. The numbers seen at each are also recorded.
- *Outcomes.* As usual, these are more difficult. Intermediate outcomes are generally calculated, so that it should be known how many of an age group have received various immunizations etc. These have to be used because there is no way of knowing how many cases of measles have been prevented.

The effectiveness of *health promotion* is difficult to measure. Even true *inputs* may be difficult to calculate, since, as we have seen, many people inside and outside the health service can contribute to health promotion, and dedicated health promotion staff may spend much of their time supporting these other workers. Collecting comparable data on *processes* presents problems too. For example, how should group work with ten people be recorded, compared with work with 20, individual work and broadcasting on local radio? *Outcomes* are predominantly long term, and intermediate outcomes may be difficult to document. Objectives may include increased knowledge and changed attitudes leading to altered behaviour, but often these are hard to monitor. Even if health behaviour does not immediately change for the better after participation in a health promotion initiative, this may not represent total failure. Most changes are the result of many factors, and this health promotion experience may be necessary but not sufficient on its own.

We are still in the era in which much basic work remains to be done in developing tools for the comparison of different sorts of public health, health promotion and prevention work, and the evaluation of their effectiveness. In some places a start has been made by identifying particular outcomes to be aimed for in the year ahead and documenting the work done to forward them, as well as the position one year later. We need to make progress on this, because of the great potential of the population approach to improving health.

The effectiveness of high-risk individual versus population approaches to prevention

An issue frequently debated is whether it is better to concentrate preventive efforts on individuals at high risk of developing a particular disease or diseases, or whether it is better to direct efforts at the whole population. Health professionals used to dealing with individuals often intuitively prefer the former – there may seem little point on an individual level in spending precious time and resources on individuals who are at low risk. However, from a public health perspective we are interested in lowering the rates of disease in the whole population; to put it in epidemiological terms, our aim is to reduce the incidence of disease. For some diseases, concentrating efforts on only high-risk individuals is a very ineffective way of reducing the incidence in the population. This is illustrated below with the example of serum cholesterol and coronary heart disease.

A large American study of over 12,000 middle-aged men (the Multiple Risk Factor Intervention Study) showed that levels of serum cholesterol predicted the chances of subsequent death from coronary heart disease (CHD). When the results were graphed, the curve was found to be steeper at the higher end, and for men with serum cholesterol levels above 7.5 millimoles per litre, the death rate from CHD was 20 per 1000 men per year, compared with under 5 per 1000 per year for men with the lowest serum cholesterol levels. The natural clinical response to this is to see the priority for preventing deaths from CHD as being to focus on those men with the highest levels. Geoffrey Rose (see Further Reading), a professor of medicine turned epidemiologist, looked more closely at the data. He calculated that only 8 per cent of all the CHD deaths occurred in the highest risk group. Their personal risk was high, but their numbers were few. In fact men whose levels lay between the modal value of 5.5 and the upper level of 7.5 experienced 63 per cent of the CHD deaths. The fact that they can be at lower risk but account for more cases than the high-risk men is simply a reflection that their numbers are much greater. So, whether or not the high-risk men were successfully treated, any substantial reduction in population death rates depends on interventions to influence the levels of far more people, indeed on shifting the population mean downwards.

As we discussed previously, the community effectiveness of a treatment service depends not only on the service being effective on an individual level but also on the proportion of the people in the population with the particular health problem who are receiving the service. The situation is analogous here. To be effective on a community level, the preventive measure needs to cover the majority of people who would otherwise develop the disease. If identification of individuals at high risk only covers a small proportion of those in the population who develop the disease, then on a population level the intervention will not be very effective, irrespective of how effective it is on an individual level.

Turning knowledge on efficacy and effectiveness into better services

We have seen that good research can determine whether interventions are beneficial (efficacious) and that well designed and delivered services can effectively reach the individuals and communities who need them. Now we need to ask whether service providers are generally aware of relevant research findings? If they are, are they both taking them up and ensuring that they are only implemented for the appropriate patients? What is the evidence?

In almost every instance investigated, it has been found that the level of use of new interventions (and sometimes old ones too) varies widely between services, and even between different professionals in one service. Use Exercise 11.5 to think through why this might be.

You are aware that recent research has shown that a new method of treatment of leg ulcers is much more effective that previous methods. You visit a hospital a friend is working in and are surprised to find the old methods still in use. You try to find out why. What sort of responses might you get?

Unawareness or misreading of the research findings, distrust of research, resistance to change and financial constraints are among the factors that might be behind lack of change in response to research findings on effectiveness. Factors such as a desire to try something new on the part of either patient or care staff, failure to work out the benefit : disbenefit ratio and even payment by item of service might be behind inappropriate overuse.

Let us look at examples of each in turn, starting with inappropriateness and then examining delays.

Inappropriate use. Recent studies of cardiac surgery in both the USA and the UK found that, compared with current evidence-based guidelines, about one in seven patients experiencing coronary artery bypass grafting had been inappropriately treated, and nearly one in three had only equivocal indications for surgery. The 'inappropriateness ratio' varied from hospital to hospital, and applied to all age groups. Was this a response to the pressure to 'do something' without due consideration of the balance of risks and likely benefits?

Delays in change. Delay in the diffusion and adoption of effective interventions has a long history, and it still persists today. Researchers have found that review articles and textbooks are slow to include many important advances in the treatment of heart attack (myocardial infarction), and slow to exclude things shown to be ineffective or harmful. Some sorts of things seem to get in more quickly than others; for example, beta-blocking drugs, which had been promoted by heavy advertising campaigns. The value of appropriate rehabilitation programmes, by contrast, was very slow to get included. Perhaps too many mass communications, with frequent reports of treatment trials, some contradictory, are part of the problem. Meta-analyses are seen by experts as the answer. Health professionals will have to become more statistically sophisticated, and meta-analysts more reader-friendly, if these are to realize their full potential.

Diffusing knowledge is helpful, but it is not the same thing as changing behaviour. Practice guidelines or even mandatory instructions have long been laid down by managers or professional organizations for some health workers, such as midwives, but these are not always well received, as they may not be derived from research-based best practice. Similarly, some recent guidelines produced for doctors by 'consensus conferences' have been dubious, the product of the lowest common denominator on which the great and the good of the profession could agree. These rather discredited the idea of guidelines, but they should be rehabilitated now that meta-analysis allows reliable research-based guidelines to be drawn up. There is also research available on how best to turn good guidelines into changes in practice. For example, in one experiment in Ontario, six hospitals were just sent guidelines through the post; four other hospitals after discussion agreed to audit the implementation of the guidelines and have feedback meetings. In another four hospitals the senior doctors were asked to identify their local opinion leader. The doctors identified were given training and then embarked on work with local colleagues in identifying any problems seen in the guidelines and working through them, customizing the guidelines for local use. All methods produced some changes in practice, but the greatest changes were in the hospitals where the local opinion leader was involved. A meta-analysis of 59 published evaluations of the implementation of clinical guidelines showed these findings to be widely applicable. The probability of effective uptake of guidelines was increased if there was *local input*, *specific educational intervention* and an additional point, *specific* reminders at the time the relevant activity was to be carried out.

Mass communications can reach and influence other groups too, including patients and other service users. Professionals know that hysterectomy rates vary widely, and generally are rising. There is no evidence, however, that women living in areas with higher rates are benefiting from the extra surgery. In a case–control study in the only Italian-speaking canton in Switzerland, these variations were widely publicized and discussed in the Italian language newspapers, TV and radio. Two months later hysterectomy rates in the canton began to fall, falling 26 per cent in a year, against a 57 per cent rise in the previous five years. Elsewhere in Switzerland, the control area, the rise continued.

Closing the loop

What can we learn from examining effectiveness? One lesson is that health knowledge does not stand still and that the potential to do good or harm continues to grow. Another is that evaluation of practice is difficult, but that there is new evidence, based on new techniques, to guide us. As professionals we can use evidence from research and from documenting our own services to complete the feedback loop and improve the effectiveness of our own practice.

Summary

Address the following questions to help you write a short summary to this chapter.

1 How do efficacy and effectiveness differ?

2 Give a 'checklist' of factors to consider when evaluating the effectiveness of a health service.

3 Discuss the strengths and weaknesses of different kinds of health service information available to help to evaluate effectiveness.

4 Distinguish between community (population) effectiveness and effectiveness on an individual level. Give examples.

5 Describe measures you might take to ensure that up-to-date research information on effectiveness is used by a hospital or primary health care team to improve their services.

FURTHER READING

Chapter 1

Ash, J.S.A., Cole, S.K. and Kilbane, P.J. (1991) Health information resources: United Kingdom – health and social factors, in W.W. Holland, K. Detels and G. Knox (eds) *Oxford Textbook of Public Health*, 2nd edn. Oxford: Oxford University Press, pp. 29–53.

Knox, E.G. (1991) Information needs in public health, in W.W. Holland, R. Detels and G. Knox (eds) *Oxford Textbook of Public Health*, 2nd edn. Oxford: Oxford University Press, pp. 3–9.

Chapters 2 to 5

Buck, C., Llopis, A., Najera, E. and Terris, M. (eds) (1988) *The Challenge of Epidemiology: Issues and Selected Readings*. Washington DC: Pan American Health Organization. (For a rich collection of 'classic' epidemiological studies.)

Hennekens, C.H. and Buring, J.E. (1987) *Epidemiology in Medicine*. Boston: Little, Brown and Co. (For clearly described epidemiological theory.)

Last, J.M. (1988) *A Dictionary of Epidemiology*. Oxford: Oxford University Press. (For definitions of epidemiological terms.)

Chapter 6

Gray, A. (ed.) (1993) *World Health and Disease*. Buckingham: Open University Press.

Macintyre, S. (1994) Understanding the social patterning of health: the role of the social sciences, *Journal of Public Health Medicine*, 16(1), 53–9.

McKeown, T. (1979) *Role of Medicine: Dream, Mirage or Nemesis*. Oxford: Blackwell.

Susser, M. (1973) *Causal Thinking of the Health Sciences*. Oxford: Oxford University Press.

Wilkinson, R.G. (1993) The impact of income equality of life expectancy, in S. Platt *et al.* (eds) *Locating Health: Sociological and Other Explanations*. Aldershot: Avebury.

Chapter 7

Ashton, J. and Seymour, H. (1988) *The New Public Health*. Milton Keynes: Open University Press.

Davies, R.S., Fyfe, C. and Tannerhill, A. (1990) *Health Promotion: Models and Values*. Oxford: Oxford Medical Publications.

Ewles, L. and Simnet, I. (1995) *Promoting Health: a Practical Guide to Health Education*, 3rd edn. London: Bailliere Tindall.

World Health Organization (1986) Ottawa charter for health promotion, *Journal of Health Promotion*, 1, 1–14.

Chapter 8

Bradshaw, J. (1972) The concept of social need, *New Society*, 30 March.

Council for the Education and Training of Health Visitors (1977) *An Investigation into the Principles of Health Visiting*. London: CETHV. (Gives examples of health needs and the principles of searching for needs and stimulating awareness of them.)

Higgs, Z.R. and Gustafson, D.D. (1985) *Community as a Client*. Philadelphia: F.A. Davis Co.

Luker, K. and Orr, J. (1992) *Health Visiting*. Oxford: Blackwell Scientific Publications. (Addresses definitions of a community and approaches to the assessment of community needs as well as those of the individual and family.)

Townsend, P., Phillimore, P. and Beattie, A. (1988) *Health and Deprivation*. London: Croom Helm. (Details differences and inequalities in health status in the northern region of England, using the political ward as a unit of analysis.)

Chapter 9

Barker, W. (1990) Practical and ethical doubts about screening for child abuse, *Health Visitor*, 63(1), 14–17. (Useful reference addressing the use of screening for issues that are not pathological.)

Chrystie, I. *et al.* (1992) Screening pregnant women for evidence of current hepatitis B infection: selective or universal?, *Health Trends*, 24(1), 13–15. (Gives a detailed example of the problems that could present with a selective as opposed to a mass screening programme, particularly when a problem may have a high incidence in some areas and a low incidence in other areas.)

Last, J.M. (1988) *A Dictionary of Epidemiology*. Oxford: Oxford University Press.

Martin, J. and Main, P.J. (1992) Cervical screening: default and compliance, *Health Visitor Journal*, 65(4), 123–4. (This article focuses on cervical cancer, but is concerned with identifying or offering explanations for variable uptake of screening.)

Potrykus, C. (1993) Universal screening better for children, *Health Visitor*, 66(9), 307–8. (This article provides another example of the possible impact of moving from a universal or mass screening perspective to a selective format.)

Chapters 10 and 11

Antman, E. *et al.* (1992) A comparison of the results of meta-analysis of randomised controlled trials and the recommendations of clinical experts, *Journal of the American Medical Association*, 268, 240–8.

Brook, R.H. (1994) Appropriateness: the next frontier, *British Medical Journal*, 308, 218–19.

Buckman, R. and Lewith, G. (1994) What does homeopathy do – and how? *British Medical Journal*, 309, 103–6.

Cochrane, A. (1972) *Effectiveness and Efficiency: Random Reflections on Health Services.* London: Nuffield Provincial Hospital Trust. (Classic early review of the need for and difficulties of evaluation.)

Donabedian, A. (1988) The quality of care: how can it be assessed?, *Journal of the American Medical Association*, 260, 1743–8. (Introduces the concepts of input, process and outcome.)

Illich, I. (1975) *Medical Nemesis: The Expropriation of Health.* London: Calder and Boyars.

McKeown, T. (1976) *The Modern Rise of Population.* London: Edward Arnold. (Reviews the evidence about the impact of clinical medicine on changes in population health.)

Mosteller, F. (1981) Innovation and evaluation, *Science*, 211, 881–6. (Documents the scurvy story and discusses the general issue of the spread of innovations.)

Rose, G. (1992) *The Strategy of Preventive Medicine.* Oxford: Oxford University Press.

St-Leger, A.S., Schneiden, H. and Walsworth-Bell, J.P. (1992) *Evaluating Health Services' Effectiveness.* Buckingham: Open University Press. (Discusses principles and how to do it.)

Tudor-Hart, J. (1988) *A New Kind of Doctor.* London: Merlin. (Reports studies on failure to implement research findings effectively.)

INDEX